Introduction

W elcome to A Celebration of Hand-Hooked Rugs XIV. Each year for the past 14 years Rug Hooking magazine has published the finest 30 rugs, narrowed down from a field of over 130 entries by four respected judges, chosen for their expertise in the rug hooking community. Their task is daunting—to jury slides submitted by each applicant and to fairly rate the rugs based on color, execution, design, or interpretation of design. The results shown on the pages of this edition represent the best selected from this year's group of applicants.

This has been a year of firsts here at Rug Hooking—my first year as editor, my first experience with the Celebration contest, a new slide process for the judges, and new changes to the book itself. What excitement to find myself surrounded by these beautiful rugs and to be immersed in the process of choosing this year's winners. Being exposed to the rugs and the talented people who hook them is not only an inspiration, but it is a daily learning experience. After attending several shows during the past year, I'm aware of the growing popularity of rug hooking; fiber art is the perfect medium for creative expression—the tactile feel of the wool, the creative dyeing process, the fabulous colors— the variety is limitless.

For those of you familiar with the Celebration editions of the past, you'll remember that last year the Honorable Mention Gallery category was expanded to include 20 rugs from the 6 shown in previous years. The tradition continues as this year's Honorable Mention categories include Animal/Bird rugs, Floral/Nature Rugs, Oriental/Ethnic/ Geometric/Folk Art Rugs, Pictorial Rugs, and Primitive/Wide-Cut Rugs.

We are also adding an additional 16 pages to Celebration, making it a total of 96 pages. Besides featuring the winners, we are includ-

contest; the second explaining the judging process from the perspective of a recent judge; and the third on decorating with hooked rugs featuring the home of Peggy Hannum.

Our look has changed and the book has expanded, but our goal is to bring as much value and pleasure to our readers as we can. Take time to relax and study the remarkable photographs of the winning rugs and the inspiration behind each one. Every story has a depth of meaning, which not only changes the way you view the winning entries, but also enhances knowledge of how this incredible art form can be used for creative expression.

Now it's your turn to judge these Celebration rugs. Simply tear out the enclosed Readers' Choice Ballot, pick your favorite three rugs in each category— Original Designs and Commercial Designs or Adaptations—along with one rug in each of the Honorable Mention categories, and **mail it back to us by or before December 31, 2004.** The winners will appear in next year's June/July/August issue of Rug Hooking magazine. If you have a special rug you would like to enter in next year's contest, look in the November/December 2004 and the January/February 2005 issues of Rug Hooking to learn how to apply for Celebration XV.

On a personal note, I enjoy viewing each and every rug and want you to know how delighted I am to be a part of your world. Now get ready to turn the page and enjoy the rugs of Celebration XIV.

—Ginny Stimmel

On the Cover: Cecille Caswell's creation, Dance of Life, exudes energy and her zest for living. See page 58 to learn more about Cecille and her rug.

The Celebration Icon: This year's Celebration icon, Caswell Fruit, is hooked by Sheri Bennett. The original of this beautiful circa 1830s rug adaptation is currently on display in the Metropolitan Museum of Art. See page 16 to learn more about Caswell Fruit.

Table of Contents

COMMERCIAL DESIGNS OR ADAPTATIONS

ORIENTAL/ETHNIC/GEOMETRIC/FOLK ART RUGS

HONORABLE MENTION GALLERY

ANIMAL/BIRD RUGS

FLORAL/NATURE RUGS

Meet the Judges

FROM LEFT TO RIGHT: *Ginny Stimmel (Editor of* Celebration *and* Rug Hooking*), Lisa McMullen (Assistant Editor of* Celebration *and* Rug Hooking*), Diane Stoeffel, Pat Cross, Sandra Brown, Lea McCrone, and Romayne Leedy (*Celebration *Assistant).*

Moving up our publication date for *A Celebration of Hand-Hooked Rugs XIV* also meant moving the date for the contest judging. Usually held in mid-March, this year it was held in mid-February and we all waited with anticipation to see if the precarious Pennsylvania winter would cooperate. Amazingly, it did, and our judges made it to Central Pennsylvania without a hitch. And the dates weren't the only things we changed—our venue was new and how we viewed the slides was different too. So, on a cold, Friday the 13th, our discriminating judges set forth to choose from the over 134 entries the winning 30 rugs you see here, along with 23 honorable mentions.

But one thing didn't change, our talented judges represent the world of rug hooking in all its many dimensions—from wide-cut primitives to finely shaded rugs, some teach, some write books—but they all share a great love for their fiber art. Read on to learn more about them.

SANDRA BROWN.
While growing up in the Midwest Sandra was influenced by her family's artistic tendencies and after attending high school in the Orient and learning sewing and crewel embroidery, she obtained a degree in art history and later a Master's in Asian Art History. Sandra began rug hooking in 1981 when a hooking group demonstrated at a local historical society. She credits Charlotte Price as her mentor who also encouraged Sandra to get McGown teacher training. Sandra has garnered awards ranging from Best of Show at Sauder Village to four appearances in *A Celebration of Hand-Hooked Rugs*. In addition to her teaching activities, she has patented the Pittsburgh Crafting Frame and began manufacturing them out of her basement, an undertaking she calls the "bread and butter" of her rug hooking business.

PAT CROSS.
Pat has been hooking and designing rugs for 12 years developing a unique primitive style that makes her rugs look like antiques. Pat's new book, *Purely Primitive: Hooked Rugs from Wool, Yarn and Homespun Scraps* (Martingale Publishing, 2003) has become a favorite among rug hookers striving for that same look. Pat is the current historian for the Association of Traditional Hooking Artists and teaches at many camps and workshops, including the Green Mountain Rug School and Shenandoah Valley Rug Retreat. She has written articles on dyeing and scrappy rugs for *Rug Hooking*. Pat resides in Charlottesville, Virginia, with her husband Tom and their "girls", Emma and Scout (their cats).

LEA McCRONE.
Lea, a part-time orthopedic home care nurse, hails from Malvern, Pennsylvania, where she is the owner of the L.M. collection—a small clothing, jewelry, and gift business. She is also the co-owner of Wool n' Tiques. Lea has been hooking for 15 years and still uses her grandmother's Rigby cutter. Her rugs have appeared three times in *A Celebration of Hand-Hooked Rugs* and she has won 3rd place in the 2003 People's Choice Awards at the Brandywine Rug Hooking Guild show. She frequently designs many of her rugs using family and pets for inspiration.

DIANE STOFFEL.
Diane started hooking 28 years ago and six years later became a McGown certified teacher. Throughout her teaching career Diane has continually extended her art background through coursework and training, including classes with Maryanne Lincoln who helped Diane learn all about color. She has been teaching for 13 years at rug camps, in adult education classes, and in her home in Brewster, Massachusetts. Her rugs have been awarded first prize in many state and county fairs and have been featured in *Rug Hooking* and its precursor *Rug Hooking News and Views*. Diane is very proud that some of her students have become accomplished rug hookers, including several who have been featured in *A Celebration of Hand-Hooked Rugs* and in *Rug Hooking.—Lisa McMullen*

2004 EDITION
A CELEBRATION OF
HAND-HOOKED RUGS XIV

Editor
Virginia P. Stimmel

Assistant Editor
Lisa McMullen

Celebration Assistant
Romayne Leedy

Designer
CW Design Solutions, Inc.

Rug Photography
Impact Xpozures

Advertising Manager
Diana Marcum

Chairman
M. David Detweiler

Publisher
J. Richard Noel

A Publication of

R·U·G
HOOKING

1300 Market St., Suite 202
Lemoyne, PA 17043-1420
(717) 234-5091
(800) 233-9055
www.rughookingonline.com
rughook@paonline.com

Printed in China
ISBN 1-881982-40-8

A Brief History

T he art of rug hooking is centuries old, although just how old is debatable. Theories abound regarding when and where the craft actually started. Some historians believe that descendants of the ancient Egyptians made the first hand-hooked rugs between the third and seventh centuries. Others maintain that rug hooking originated in China or Europe.

We do know for certain, however, that rug hooking experienced a major resurgence of interest in the mid-19th century in New England and the Maritime Provinces of Canada. Born initially out of necessity, hand-hooked rugs were created by rural women to cover the bare floors of their homes. Later, people began selling hand-hooked rugs, and cottage industries eventually sprang up across the continent.

By the 1940s, rug hooking had become a well-established hobby in the United States and Canada. It has evolved into a popular means of personal expression as well as a practical pastime. Hand-hooked rugs can be found on the walls of art galleries from New York City and Washington, D.C. to Tokyo and London, as well as in museums, office buildings, libraries, and cultural centers across North America.

Picture Perfect

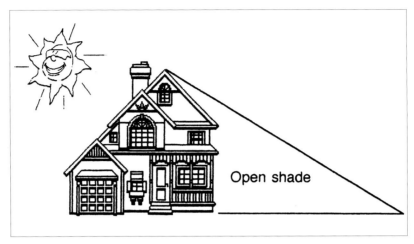

Open shade

You've hooked a beautiful rug and now you want to show it off. But the gallery or curator of an exhibit won't accept your rug until they see slides of it. You want to take the photographs yourself but doubt your abilities to show your rug in its best light. You had a teacher to help with all your hooking questions, but who do you go to now for a photography lesson?

For almost 17 years, Bill Bishop, owner of Impact Xpozures, has been the main photographer for *Rug Hooking* magazine, *A Celebration of Hand-Hooked Rugs* and many of our books. He received his BFA degree in commercial photography from the prestigious Rochester Institute of Technology in Rochester, New York. With that background we thought he would be the perfect person to explain how to get terrific photos of your hooked work.

USING THE RIGHT EQUIPMENT

According to Bill, your slides will only be as good as the equipment you use to take them. Literally hundreds of styles of 35-millimeter cameras exist, from the fully automatic, which focus and set the shutter speed and lens opening for you; to fully manual models, which require you to make all of the settings; to ones with a combination of these features. For good quality slides, Bill recommends using a camera that allows you to adjust at least the lens opening and the focus. Automatic, point-and-shoot cameras do not give you enough control over the exposure. If you don't have such a camera, try and borrow one from a friend or relative making sure you familiarize yourself with how the camera works before taking any pictures.

Slide film is available in different speeds, just as point film is. Ektachrome 200 is a good choice for color slides. (The exception to using Ektachrome 200 occurs if you are taking pictures inside

with only incandescent bulbs for lighting—read on for more information.)

If you are taking slides indoors, a flash is probably necessary. An ordinary flash for a 35-millimeter camera is perfectly adequate. A tripod is probably not required for you to take good slides if the lighting is adequate.

THE BEST LIGHTING

For best results, Bill recommends photographing your rug outdoors, however, not in direct sunlight. Rather, photograph in open shade without a flash. The side of your house directly opposite the sun is in open shade (see sketch). Take your shots between 10 a.m. and 2 p.m. Later on the shade will be too cool and your photographs will have a blue tint.

If you can't photograph your rug outdoors, use a flash and shoot indoors, preferably near a large window or other source of natural light. If you must turn on additional lamps, make sure they are not fluorescent. Using incandescent lamps as your only light source (no flash) is not recommended, but if you must, use Ektachrome tungsten film in your camera. This film is balanced to compensate for the inconsistency of incandescent color. You may also purchase a couple of quartz lamps at a hardware store to light your rug. Using these lamps along with tungsten film will give you good results.

SETTING UP THE SHOT

Do not photograph your rug by pointing the camera down onto it as it lies on the floor. Even a small rug will lose its shape in the frame because you can't get directly over the rug without including your feet in the shot. The best way to photograph your rug is to

USING A MANUAL CAMERA

Cameras work by exposing light-sensitive film to an image that passes through the lens of the camera. A manual camera allows you to adjust the focus, the shutter speed (which determines how quickly the shutter opens and closes), and the lens opening (which determines how much light enters the lens). In a very bright scene, the lens opening needs to be small and the shutter speed fast so that too much light does not strike the film, resulting in overexposure. Conversely, in a dark scene the lens opening needs to be large and the shutter speed slow so that adequate light can reach the film to prevent underexposure.

Manual cameras determine the correct settings for the shutter speed and lens opening with a light meter. Light meters measure the average amount of light striking the lens. Depending on the camera, the light meter may take the form of a floating needle (like a speedometer needle) or a blinking light that is visible in the viewfinder. Make sure you know how the light meter works.

The shutter speed is usually set with a knob on the top of the camera. Most film containers provide information on the best shutter speed to use for that particular film speed. Information is also given for shutter speeds in different lighting conditions and with or without a flash.

The lens opening is set by turning a diaphragm ring on the lens. This is the first numbered ring closest to the body of the camera. Each of the numbers on the ring corresponds to an f-stop, which is a fraction. Therefore, the higher the number, the smaller the lens opening. If you remove the lens from the camera and look at the back of it, you will see the lens opening increase or decrease as you turn the ring. To decrease the amount of light entering the lens, turn the ring to the right as you hold the camera. To increase the light, turn the ring to the left. Rotate the ring until the light meter indicates that the proper setting has been achieved.

The next two numbered rings on the lens are the depth of field guide and the focus ring. The focus ring is turned to bring the subject into focus and the depth of field guide indicates the range of distance that is in focus at each setting.

You don't have to be a mechanical genius to operate a manual camera; adjusting the settings takes only seconds. Being able to control the shutter speed and lens opening ensures good results even under less than ideal conditions.

hang it up. If shooting outside, nail a carpet tack strip to your garage door or outside wall. The tacks will grip the back of your rug on a white or light wall to photograph it.

Another option is to prop up a sheet of plywood or cardboard at an

Outside example

angle, cover it with a white sheet, and lay your rug on it. Stand on a stepladder and shoot directly down onto the rug. This will enable you to get the plane of the lens parallel to the plane of the rug, as it would be if the rug were hanging on a wall.

When you are looking through the viewfinder, make sure there are no other objects in the frame except your rug. Then make sure there are no bright spots or shadows on it.

Get as close to the rug as you can so that it fills as much of the frame as possible (but keep the rug in focus). To shoot close-ups, you should be no more than 1 ¹/₂ to 2 feet away from the rug. (A close-up means you are closer to the rug than when you took the shot of the entire rug. It does not mean photographing just a part of the rug from the same distance.)

BRACKETING SHOTS

A camera's light meter doesn't always give you the best exposure because it measures the average amount of light striking the lens. To compensate, Bill recommends bracketing—making several exposures of the same shot at different lens openings. For each image you need, take four or five exposures. Making multiple exposures is the best way to ensure that you get decent slides of your rug.

To bracket a shot, begin by making an exposure at the f-stop indicated by the light meter. Then make an exposure at each of the two f-stops lower than the original shot, and at each of the two f-stops higher than the original. For example, if the light meter indicates the proper exposure is at f-stop 5.6, make one exposure there and then one exposure each at f-stops 8, 11, 4, and 2.8.

After the film is developed, you will have five possibilities to choose from for each shot. This may seem like a waste of film, but it's the best way to ensure successful results. If you take only one shot and it's too dark or washed out, you're stuck with it. A bonus

Inside example

is that if several shots are good, you'll have extra slides of your rug for contests or for your personal use.

Many photo shops send slide film to an off-site lab to be processed, so you may wait two weeks or more for your slides. Therefore, allow extra time if you need the slides back by a certain date.

If you follow these suggestions, you should get decent results when photographing your rugs. The key is to use a good camera, good lighting, and a good dose of common sense. With this combination, you'll get good slides every time. ∎

A Judge's Perspective

BY PAT CROSS

LEFT: *Example of overexposed lighting—the rug loops, color, or execution cannot properly be seen.*

BOTTOM RIGHT: *Example of overexposed lighting—the finishing techniques or consistency of hooking on the back of the rug cannot be determined.*

After my first experience as a judge for *A Celebration of Hand-Hooked Rugs*, I thought more of you would like to know exactly how the judging process works. I bet you thought the judges knew who hooked each entry—wrong. To this day I don't know the names of the people who hooked the rugs. It is a completely anonymous process.

I arrived in Harrisburg, Pennsylvania, the day before the judging. That evening the four judges, Ginny Stimmel (Editor), Lisa McMullen (Assistant Editor), Romayne Leedy (*Celebration* Assistant), and Richard Noel (Publisher) met in the lobby of the Hampton Inn and carpooled to dinner. We dined in a beautiful timber-framed building that was part of a new golf course community. The atmosphere was very relaxed, dinner was delicious, and the conversation was casual. After dinner we returned to the Hampton Inn and retired for the evening.

THE PROCESS

Judging began at 8:30 the next morning in a small conference room at the hotel. Envision tables set up in a U-shaped fashion and at the bottom of the U were four slide projectors. Lisa and Romayne operated two projectors each. On either side of the U sat two judges with Ginny off to the side by herself. On the table in front of each judge was a notebook divided into two categories, original designs and commercial designs or adaptations, and two sections, first round and second round of judging. The *only* information on these pages was the title of the rug and its dimensions. There were *no* names. If any additional information was given, it was presented by Ginny at the time each set of slides appeared on the screen. This additional information might pertain to something as simple as what the rug was adapted from or whose commercial pattern it was. Nothing was ever said that gave us a hint as to whose rug it was.

Four slides of each rug were shown—one of the entire rug, two showing details and one of the finished edges. Original designs

LEFT: *Example of overexposed rug shot with washed out color.*

were judged on color, execution, and originality of design. Commercial designs or adaptations were judged on color, execution and interpretation of design.

The judging system was all by numbers. We graded each rug by the three criteria noted above and total high scores won. It was that simple. The grading was from 1 (poor) to 5 (excellent). There was no 3 as we *weren't* allowed to wimp out and pick a noncommittal, middle of the road number.

This year there were 134 rugs entered in the competition and were about equally divided between the original and commercial design categories. We were instructed that there would be no talking among the judges. If we wanted a little extra time to look at the slides, we could request that. The process I'm about to explain was done for each category. So let the judging begin—lights out.

We began with a quick run through of the original design entries using only the projector that contained slides of the entire rug. This was done so we had an idea of what was coming. Next all four slides of each rug appeared on the screen at the same time. (Now you see why there were four projectors.) Presenting the slides this way was great because we could see everything at once and didn't have to flip back and forth.

Below each entry in the notebook we circled a number along side the criteria they were being judged on—color, execution, and originality of design. We were also asked to tally our scores and enter the total score for each rug. The lowest total score a rug could receive was 3 and the highest was 15. We did this for each rug in the original design category.

When we completed the original design category, we took a break. This was an opportunity to stretch our legs, visit the powder room, or get another cup of coffee for the second half of the first round of judging. No one discussed the rugs we had just seen.

Again the lights were turned out and we proceeded exactly as we had done before, but this time we were viewing the entries in the commercial designs or adaptations category. When we finished with this round, the lights were turned back on and we were asked for the total score for each rug in both categories. We started with the very first rug in the original design category and continued until we finished with the last rug in the commercial designs or adaptations category. The title of a rug was called out by Ginny and each judge took turns calling out the total score we had given that particular rug. We were finally allowed to speak, but only to give a number that ranged from 3 to 15.

Now it was lunchtime—but only for the judges and Ginny. Lisa and Romayne stayed behind to WORK. It was their job to find the top 25 rugs in each category. Once they did that, they removed all

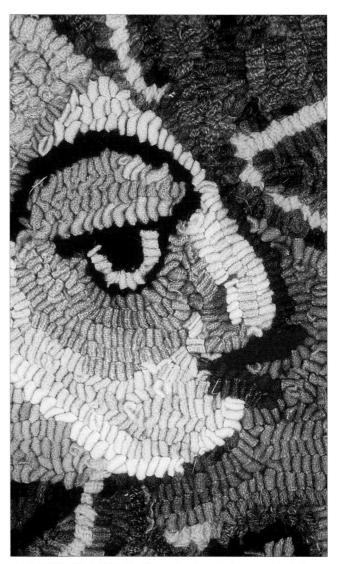

A GOOD CLOSE-UP: *Example of good close-up detail shot of rug shown above left. Note variation in color between both samples.*

of the slides that didn't make the cut. They rearranged the slides in the four slide projectors and wrote the titles of these rugs on the pages of part two of our notebooks while the rest of us relaxed, ate, and talked, but not about the rugs.

We returned with lunch for Lisa and Romayne and were ready for round number two which was exactly like round one, but there were fewer rugs to judge. Again, we got a quick preview of the rugs in each category, then viewed all four slides of each rug for the second time and judged them. We went through both categories, tallied our scores, and again stated our totals.

During the final round of judging we were given some additional time to write personal comments about the rugs in the notebooks below the total score for each rug. Some of these comments have been extracted from the judge's notebooks and are included in the section "In the Judge's Words" that you see here.

The top 15 rugs in each category are featured and the remaining 20 are highlighted under honorable mention. All 50 are WINNERS.

MY THOUGHTS

Judging was a simple process—circle a number and add them up—high score wins, but it wasn't exactly that simple. I have entered the competition before and received that rejection letter. It hurts. For those of you who have gotten one, you have to remember that judging is so subjective. It's based on total scores from four different judges.

After all the numbers were totaled and the judging was completed, we did talk amongst ourselves. We didn't look at slides and discuss them individually, but we'd throw out things like—"You know that rug that had such and such—why did you give it a mediocre score of 8 when the rest of us gave it a 15?" The differences in what each judge saw, or what influenced us were amazing. For me, no one lost. There were just some rugs that wowed us more than others.

Along the way I had to make a couple of decisions about my personal judging. First I decided that no one would get a score of 1 in any category. I felt that each entrant made the effort to hook the rug, take the slides, and enter, so regardless of how the color, execution, or original the design was, they started out with a 2 from me in each category or a minimal score of 6.

The hardest judgment call I had to make was based on the slides. I saw some of these rugs at the ATHA Biennial in Charlotte, North Carolina and I knew what the real rug looked like. To be fair to all involved, I decided to judge each rug based on the slides submitted, and the poor quality of slides is the reason some rugs didn't make the cut. I suggest you read the article, *Picture Perfect (on page 6)* before you take or have slides taken.

In the future when you submit a rug, here are a few hints that might help you make the cut. When you review the slides you're

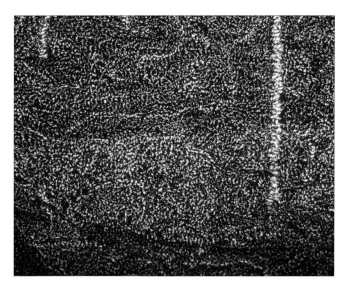

A GOOD CLOSE-UP: *An example of a good close-up detail shot.*

submitting, is the color the same in all of them? We had one entry where the color of the rug appeared gray in the full view, but blue in the close ups. The gray blob ruined what may have been a beautiful rug. What color was that rug?

Workmanship must be topnotch and I'm talking about finishing. You wouldn't believe how some of those rugs were finished. One actually was submitted with just the burlap turned to the back. Who knows what the rest of the rug looked like because the slide of the finished edge was like a neon sign that distracted us from seeing the quality in the rest of the rug.

Design is also very important. Look at it critically. Are there huge empty spaces, is it cluttered and unbalanced? This applies to commercial patterns too. One rug in particular appeared top heavy with sky, whereas another had a center motif with way too much space around it.

There were 134 rugs with four slides each. Some of the slides were great and some were very bad. Some of the rugs just wowed us regardless of our personal preference in hooking. Many of you have complained that there aren't enough primitive rugs and there are too many fine cut rugs. Stop and think about what we had to judge. There were very few primitive entries, so we could only present to you the best of what was shown to us.

Others mention that some people's rugs always seem to make it into *Celebration*. The secret is out—they enter and present nice slides, do beautifully finished work, and they make the cut. If you don't enter, you can't be selected. Yes, there were four judges and we have personal tastes, but the people at *Rug Hooking* work hard to make sure we're a diverse group so the judging gives everyone a fair chance.

My advice to everyone who wants to enter is to plan ahead. Work on a rug every year that you think is worthy of entering. Allow enough time to take and maybe retake slides so they show your rug off well and finish your rug so no judge can find fault. ■

SHOWCASE OF

Commercial Designs and Adaptations

Review these pages carefully, then mark and mail the ballot inserted into this book to vote for the rugs you consider the best of the best. For more information on how these rugs were selected, and how the Readers'-Choice Contest is run, see page 1.

American Star

Whenever Debby Cooper would flip through the pages of her large collection of folk art books for ideas and inspiration, there was a particular picture of an antique crocheted afghan that she kept returning to time and again. The exciting colors and back-to-back flags and eagle evoked strong feelings of patriotism and she loved the complicated patterns. "It had the added bonus of wonderful geometrics," Debby recalls. "I wanted to hook it."

Even though the basic design was in a book, Debby wanted to give her rug some originality and a style all its own. In order to do that, she decided that the rug's main colors would be red, blue, gold, and green. Once she determined her colors, she was confronted with the challenge of finding textured wool in the same color families and then hooking them in opposing designs. She began putting the shades together creating exciting contrasts and was able to do the geometrics in the border without clashing the colors. "My teacher, Jule Marie Smith, taught me to trust my eye and I found that I enjoyed putting colors together that others wouldn't think matched," Debby says.

Because fumes from dyeing wool bother her, Debby was able to get the wool she needed for *American Star* from her teachers who used the open pot method, scrunch and spot method, and overdyeing of textures which gave the rug an antique look. Debby's favorite parts of the rug are the flags because she loves the colors used in the white stripes and the different backgrounds. She also used various shades of beige on each flag and hooked in green for one background and periwinkle for the other. To finish the edges and avoid bulkiness of this linen-backed rug, Debby used binding tape and then utilized strips of the dark blue border wool to cover the edges. She then cut on the bias and sewed the ends together at an angle, turned them under and stitched them down.

American Star is proudly displayed within the staircase hallway of Debby's house in Houston. It showcases Debby's original rug hooking style but at the same time pays homage to the originality of the antique crocheted afghan that inspired her.

DEBBY COOPER
HOUSTON, TEXAS

When Debby Cooper couldn't find a hooked rug she liked for her kitchen and the cost of commissioning one proved too high, she decided to learn rug hooking and found she loved it. Since 1996, Debby has hooked 26 pieces, ranging from a small hooked and mounted Christmas tree to a 3' x 5' rug of a folk art pig, and even a table runner commemorating her father's 50 years as a minister. She prefers hooking primitives using wide cut wool on linen and most of her projects are her own designs with some adaptations of antiques. And, oh yes, Debby finally does have a hooked rug in her kitchen—one that she created herself.

In the Judges' Words

"NICE PRIMITIVE COLORS—SUBTLE. BEAUTIFULLY FINISHED."

"NICE BALANCE AND COLORS."

American Star, 26" x 33", #8-cut wool on linen, adapted from an antique crocheted afghan, 2003.

Caswell Fruit

Sheri Bennett's definite opinions about what colors she picks for her home décor made *Caswell Fruit* a perfect choice for her next rug hooking project. "I truly love the color red and this rug gave me plenty of places to use it," says Sheri. "I worked closely with my teacher, Ramona Maddox, on the color palette. She doesn't try to steer me in directions I don't want to go."

Caswell Fruit is an adaptation of an antique rug based upon an original rug made in the early 1830s presently on display in the Metropolitan Museum of Art. "The section my rug was copied from was made to be removed in the winter to protect it from sparks from the fireplace," Sheri explains. "The original rug measures 159" x 147"." Sheri was attracted to the smaller section

because of her love for antiques. She also felt that the large motifs would translate well in the larger cuts she likes to use and, as a quilter, she is often drawn to patterns that contain baskets or fruit.

Sheri calls *Caswell Fruit* a "team effort" and notes that Ramona guided her to the perfect shades. Since Sheri had no wool dyeing experience but hopes to learn in the near future, Ramona abrashed and spot-dyed the wool used for the rug's background, and most of the fruit and flowers, while new and recycled wool was used for the rest. At first, Sheri felt intimidated by all the grapes and strawberries in the design but she found them fun to do as she worked on them a little at a time. Although it was tedious to put the seeds in the strawberries, she was surprised that the fruit turned out to be her favorite part of the

SHERI BENNETT

CORBIN, KENTUCKY

Sheri Bennett started hooking rugs in 1996 and literally goes to great lengths to pursue her fiber art obsession. For the past five years, she has traveled three hours each way to classes from her small southeastern Kentucky town to Chattanooga, Tennessee. "I look forward to the drive each week that classes are in session," Sheri remarks. "I know what fun awaits me at the end of the drive." To date, Sheri has completed three small rugs and two larger projects but wishes she could hook faster so she could add to that number. Her Pineapple Antique appeared in Celebration XI.

rug. For *Caswell Fruit*, Sheri hooked more freely and did not stick to the outline and fill method used in most primitive rugs.

Sheri made sure that the rug's colors would fit in nicely with any room in her Kentucky home. For now, she is considering placing *Caswell Fruit* on her living room wall.

In the Judges' Words

"NICE WORKMANSHIP AND FINISHING."

Caswell Fruit, 72 ¹/₂" x 30 ¹/₂", #6 and 8-cut wool on burlap, 2003, designed by Lib Calloway.

Charleston Sweetgrass Baskets

Many of us have baskets either as part of our home décor or simply as a utilitarian receptacle to hold odds and ends. But the sweetgrass baskets created by Charleston, South Carolina artists were the kind that Valerie Johnston had always admired and owned. The inspiration to turn these wonderful baskets into fiber art came when she saw a photograph taken by her husband, Charles, which depicted a grouping of baskets in the Charleston marketplace. Valerie immediately knew that she wanted to hook it as a wall hanging for her home but was concerned about doing justice to the photograph as well as to the real baskets.

Valerie drew the basket image onto the monk's cloth from a large black and white blow-up of the photograph. During a three-day hook-in with her rug hooking group last year, Valerie and her teacher began color planning the rug. It took a lot of color swatches before the two of them were satisfied with the color combinations. Once she was back home, Valerie had the dyeing formulas mixed and the new wool jar dyed.

The most challenging aspect of the rug for Valerie were the lids on the baskets. She wanted them to have a multi-dimensional look like you could almost lift them off the basket, which she accomplished by shading. Seeing each basket come to life was Valerie's favorite part as she began completing her project. She loved the swirl pattern in the main basket because of the color contrast that almost makes the swirl look like it is in motion.

Charleston Sweetgrass Baskets was a joy for Valerie to hook and a tribute to those who painstakingly create these beautiful crafts, as well as doing justice to her husband's photograph. The rug is now displayed in the entry hall of Valerie's home. "It is my way of thanking the artists who create these beautiful baskets and for their many hours of hard work and all the pleasure they give to people who buy them," says Valerie. "I admire the ones that I own everyday. In the future I hope to own a few more."

VALERIE JOHNSTON
WILMINGTON, NORTH CAROLINA

Valerie Johnston had been involved with needlework for 30 years, but it had always been her intention to hook at least one rug in her lifetime. That time came when, unbeknownst to her, her husband enrolled her in a one-day class that "whet her appetite" for the fiber art. Several years later Valerie began hooking in earnest, when she met a rug hooker who was trying to put together a group to promote the art. To date, Valerie has completed five rugs and prefers smaller cuts of wool because of the detail she loved when she did crewel embroidery. "I have no credentials and have never entered any competitions but I have been awarded life-long friends because of rug hooking," she says.

In the Judges' Words

"EXCELLENT WORKMANSHIP."

"LOVELY BALANCE OF GEOMETRIC FORMS AND SIMPLE COLOR SCHEME."

Charleston Sweetgrass Baskets, 33 ¹/₂" x 26 ¹/₂", #3-cut wool on monk's cloth, 2003. Adapted from a photograph by Charles Johnston.

Crown Prince

For Susan Naples, rug hooking is all about challenge. So when she noticed another fiber artist hooking *Crown Prince* and selling the pattern at the Cambria Pines Rug Camp, in Cambria, California, she knew she had to hook it.

With pattern in hand and an extensive wool inventory at her fingertips, Susan went to work on the rug but not before finding some excellent photographs of capuchin monkeys and receiving a calendar with an exquisite photograph of a leopard's head. Those detailed and intricate depictions assisted in her task of culling out just the right colors she needed from her stash.

But as Susan arrived at Cambria Pines ready to begin her project, those color choices were not carved in stone. Her rug hooking teacher sent her on a couple of searches for additional golds and browns for the leopard, and a supporting color for the monkey's turquoise attire. "We decided on swatches for the mirror, and spent a good deal of time fretting over the perfect color for the leopard's shirt," recalls Susan. "Under her expert guidance, the hooking went very quickly, and I accomplished much more at camp than I had hoped."

Susan found that the leopard's robe was the most challenging part of the rug to hook. She wanted to give it a rich, velvety appearance and spent a lot of time trying different colors and reverse hooking. Another challenge for Susan was choosing a background color—an aspect of the rug she waited to tackle until the end. "From the onset, I knew that I wanted a dark, Renaissance look for the background," she says. "However, nothing seemed to work. Someone suggested a lighter color, and I tried everything from dark brown to celery. Nothing satisfied me." Susan discovered the solution was to over dye a piece of brown wool with the bright colors found in the main motifs. As Susan began to hook this final part of the project, she knew that the choice made for the background was exactly what she had been looking for.

Susan learned that one should not limit color planning only to your own wool inventory. "Just imagine all the luscious wool you can buy when you are scouring the other classrooms for just the right piece," she says. "I learned never to overlook the details in a piece like this, and, I learned to trust myself, my knowledge and experience just a little more."

Crown Prince has been a royal winner for Susan in several competitions including a blue first place ribbon, a purple division winner ribbon, and a pewter mug at the Orange County Fair.

SUSAN NAPLES
SANTA ANA, CALIFORNIA

Ten years ago, Susan Naples was visiting family in New Hampshire and noticed the hand-hooked rugs that seemed to cover every square inch of her aunt's home. "The love and creativity of a lifetime's worth of hooking left me speechless," says Susan. "As the mother of four sons, my aunt was ecstatic that someone in the family was interested in carrying on her art and gleefully took me to the Dorr Mill store." Susan immediately purchased her first kits and tools and located a teacher upon her return to California. Most of Susan's 15 or so rugs and wall hangings have been made as gifts for family and friends.

In the Judges' Words

"THE EYES ARE GREAT. THE VELVET COAT SHINES. GREAT HOOKING."

"WONDERFUL ANIMAL EYES AND EXPRESSION ON THE MONKEY. RICH COLOR."

Crown Prince, 21 1/2" x 31 1/2", #3 and 4-cut wool on monk's cloth, 2003. Designed by Antoinette von Grone for Hues and Views, Inc.

Eighteenth-Century Fable

Fiber artists have various reasons why they choose certain commercial patterns to transform into rugs, but few can claim the intense connection felt by Patricia Seliga when she first laid eyes on *18th Century Fable*. "It was a heart-stopping pattern," Patricia recalls. "I wanted to do a large rug with lots of interest. This pattern just seemed to have tons of possibilities for color and technique."

One look at *18th Century Fable* and it's easy to conclude that this rug hooker didn't mind a few challenges. Patricia loved the large size of the piece despite her concerns about finishing such an immense project before one of her other ideas of something smaller and more doable would take over. She also looked forward to undertaking all the interesting details in the design, such as the fairies—a detail she thought might be tricky but, to her delight, seemed to "hook themselves." But with so many colors incorporated in the rug—the greens for the hillsides, the blues for the sky, the yellow branches for the border—the most challenging aspect of the rug for Patricia was making sure her project held a common color scheme. Patricia's solution to unify the rug was to use reds for the ladies' clothing but still give each their own style despite the similar shade.

Patricia hooked mostly in #5 and #6 wool cuts because she wanted a folk art look rather than fine shading details. One of the many things she learned from hooking *18th Century Fable* was estimating how much wool a large rug needs and also how to improvise when you run short. "I also learned that each little detail adds to the design," explains Patricia. "Adding something different to each critter or animal gave it a personality."

Patricia started working on the rug in September 2001, but family matters forced her to roll up the unfinished project and lay down her hooks for more than a year. After her mother became ill with cancer, she would often ask Patricia if the "big rug" was finished. It wasn't until after her mother's death in January 2003 that Patricia was able to complete *18th Century Fable*. "When I finally put it in my living room," she remarks, "I thought, 'Look, mom, I finished my big rug!'"

PATRICIA SELIGA

St. Louis, Missouri

Since the birth of her first child in 1977, Patricia Seliga has kept busy making quilts and doing cross-stitching, knitting, and needlepoint. Years later, her daughter, Jennifer, noticed a friend's mother hooking a rug and knew it would be something her mother would adore. Patricia began taking lessons from a local rug hooking teacher and, since 1999, she has had a love affair with her new craft. Patricia has completed over two dozen projects including commercial and original rugs, purses, and several pillows and likes to hook in all cuts from #3 to #10. Celebration XIV is the first contest Patricia has ever entered.

In the Judges' Words

"SOFT, INVITING—MAKES YOU WANT TO STUDY ALL PARTS OF THE RUG."

"NICELY BALANCED COLORS. THE DESIGN MOVES."

18th Century Fable, 64" x 88", #5- and 6-cut wool on monk's cloth. A Harry M. Fraser pattern, 2003.

Flowerbox

Summertime in and around Bryan Hancock's farm where she raises Quarter horses contains a slice of heaven. It is during those lazy, hazy days when she tends to her small rose garden and grows zinnias that she cuts and brings inside to brighten up her log home. So when she saw the pattern for *Flowerbox*, it seemed to be the perfect reminder of those wonderful carefree times when everything around her is in full bloom. She liked the design for its whimsy and quirkiness and was attracted to the primitively drawn houses. "You can't have anything but fun with a rug that has flowers as big as trees," says Bryan. "I couldn't wait to sit down and hook each day."

Bryan found this rug project an easy one to work on and complete. Her enthusiasm for the design and the memories it conjured up resulted in her finishing the rug in about eight weeks. She was able to hook a house or two a day and did the color planning as her work progressed using wool she already had on hand. Bryan used a lot of different colors in the rug but in order to capture the expanse of night sky in the background, she over dyed a large amount of wool in navy blue using an open pot on her stovetop. One of the decisions Bryan made was to keep the houses simple and put more detail and variety of colors in the flowers. But her biggest challenge in hooking the flowers was that she didn't want that detail and variety to dominate the rug's motif. As a result, she was careful to hook the tall lively blossoms in muted colors so they would not jump out when you first looked at the rug. Although the flowers are large and seem to almost touch the sky, her decision to make them more subdued helped to create a more uniform design so you see the whole rug instead of focusing in on just one element. Bryan finished the rug with a herringbone stitch around the edge of the linen backing and then sewed binding tape onto the back.

Flowerbox is a welcome addition to Bryan's log home where it lays on the floor in the center of her family room. Now, no matter what the weather outside, there will always be a bit of summertime all year round.

BRYAN HANCOCK
ROCKY MOUNT, NORTH CAROLINA

Bryan Hancock's interest in rug hooking started 20 years ago and was fueled by her love of antiques. A friend of her mother's was the first to show Bryan the fine art of hooking rugs and soon afterwards invited her to a rug camp. "My mother was kind enough to keep my 2- and 7-year-old girls so I could go," Bryan recalls. Since then Bryan has completed over 100 large pieces, about 25 small pieces, and a set of risers for her back stairs. She is a certified McGown-trained teacher and instructs others on the fiber art at Caraway Rug Camp in North Carolina.

In the Judges' Words

"GOOD PRIMITIVE. NICE USE OF COLOR AND TEXTURE. EVEN HOOKING AND NICELY FINISHED."

"GOOD USE OF LIGHT, BRIGHT, DARK, AND DULL."

Flowerbox, 38" x 50", #8 and 8 ¹/2 cut-wool on linen, 2003, designed by Karen Kahle.

Game Birds

lthough she takes great pleasure in creating her own designs, Dee Giel had two very good reasons why she chose to hook *Game Birds*. First, it reminded her of her many experiences hiking in and around the New Hampshire woods and mountains. Secondly, she could visualize the rug complementing her northeast home and warming the wide pine plank floor in her living room.

Dee wanted to include her own original touches and personalize the rug as much as possible. One of the ways she did that was to do her color planning based on the palette that Basil Ede, an English avian artist, used in his book *Wild Birds of America*. She also omitted the mallards depicted on the original pattern and replaced them with wild turkeys. Dee loves hooking animals and birds so she even added baby pheasants, bob-whites, ruffed grouse, and turkeys to keep them busy. She also added "little critters" like chipmunks and a snail, some mushrooms, and changed some of the leaf formations. "I enjoyed the challenge of incorporating the many colors, which fine shading allowed me to do to make the woodland birds come to life," Dee says.

It took Dee several weeks to dye the wool using a variety of techniques—spot, casserole, and dip dye-to create the effects she wanted along with recycled Pendleton plaids, some of which she over-dyed. To get the mottled effect, she used 19 yards of Woolrich in burgundy that was spot-dyed with hunter green. Carrying around all that dyed wool made it tempting for Dee to take a little bit here and there and use it for other rugs she was working on. In doing so, she had to re-dye some of the colors when she went full out to complete the project. "Luckily, I kept good records from the start of the work," Dee remarks. "Believe me, I stress this with my students strongly."

Dee has moved away from the beautiful New Hampshire mountains and that living room with the pine plank floor and is now living in sunny Florida in a home filled with antique Chinese furnishings and oriental rugs. Unfortunately, *Game Birds* does not blend in with her current décor so the rug is now stored away and only makes an occasional trip to an exhibit or show. The rug is the first hooked project that Dee has ever submitted for judging.

DEE GIEL

SEBASTIAN, FLORIDA

Dee Giel's fine arts background got her involved in oil painting, needlework, and weaving. But for the past 25 years, rug hooking has been one of her favorite forms of expression, an interest she developed after seeing a hooking demo at a heritage fair and from her mother who had hooked rugs for 10 years. Dee loves the detail work it commands and also likes color planning with her students or for her own projects and has been known to spend many happy hours in the dye pot. "My art background allows me to dye by eye, using the primaries and black," says Dee. "I can basically get or match any color I need this way."

In the Judges' Words

"SUBTLE USE OF GREYS, REDS, AND BROWNS. ALSO TEXTURES ARE USED HERE AND THERE TO PERFECT THE EFFECT.

Game Birds, 72" x 120", #3-5-cut wool on burlap, 2003. Designed by Edith Dana.

Happy Hours

Leslie A. Haynes always loved the whimsical fruit, flowers, and leaves of a crewel. It was exactly that which attracted her to the *Happy Hours* pattern when she saw it displayed two years ago at the McGown National Convention at Valley Forge. Leslie was accustomed to creating more traditional rugs with realistic and dimensional motifs in the short time she had been hooking. This "anything goes" rug would turn out to be not only a departure for her but also fun to hook because of the festive and "funky" design.

Before starting the rug project at Highlands Rug Hooking Camp in Fort Washington, Pennsylvania last year, Leslie visited her rug hooking teacher to do the color planning. They sifted through boxes of sample swatches and Leslie found several that worked well together and were exactly what she had in mind for the rug. She decided to have a light background and used a formula that resulted in a beautiful pale green hue on natural Dorr wool. Leslie then traveled to Devon, Pennsylvania, to do the dyeing in her aunt's kitchen surrounded by pots, jars, and dye books. The color choices and dyeing methods that Leslie used resulted in the soft warm colors that she wanted.

The crewel was fun to do, Leslie says, and she loved the fact that each flower, leaf, and piece of fruit had more than one color integrated into it. She also learned that using color around the rug kept it balanced. But even fun projects have their moments and

Leslie experienced one with the tree trunk, as she didn't want it to dominate other aspects of the design. "Originally, I was going to use tweeds," explains Leslie. "However, after hooking a bit of it, I hated it! Instead of introducing yet another color, I found that CF95 blended nicely and did not become the focal point of the rug but rather brought out the fruits, flowers, and leaves which is what I intended."

After the hooking was complete, Leslie used cording and whipped the rug with Paternayan virgin wool at the edges. She then used rug binding to finish it off.

Leslie's rug is now spending many "happy hours" between her living room and dining room . . . and the dogs have been trained not to lie on it.

LESLIE A. HAYNES
MECHANICSBURG, PENNSYLVANIA

After Leslie A. Haynes' mother passed away, her Aunt Miriam took her aside and urged her to carry on the family tradition of hooking rugs. "That was the beginning of times spent hooking at her house and by our lake in Maine, along with dyeing lessons, shading classes, and more," recalls Leslie. "She has shared wool, accessories, dyes and dye pots with me. The closeness and bond we have established is something I will cherish the rest of my life." Leslie is one of the founders of the Central PA Ruggers, a rug hooking guild in her community that brought together 10 rug enthusiasts.

In the Judges' Words

"SUBTLE COLORS. METICULOUS WORKMANSHIP. WOULD LIKE TO HAVE IT BY THE SIDE OF MY BED."

"BEAUTIFUL SUBTLE COLOR SCHEME. THERE IS ENOUGH VARIETY TO KEEP YOUR EYE MOVING AROUND THE PIECE."

Happy Hours, 28" x 42", #3-cut wool on rug warp, 2003. Designed by Pearl K. McGown.

Istanbul

Call it kismet or coincidence, but Peggy Hannum says she was meant to hook *Istanbul*, a pattern that originated from a birthday card mailed to Pearl McGown from a friend who was visiting the Turkish city.

Several years ago, Peggy's rug hooking teacher suggested that she hook the colorful design. Just hearing the name conjured up the mysteries and exotic aspects of the Middle East, a part of the world she and her husband have been traveling to for the past 20 years. "We lived in Jerusalem for three years recently as liaisons for the United Methodist Church," Peggy says. "We also have visited Istanbul several times in our travels." Last summer, Peggy's roommate at the McGown Northern Teachers' Workshop had some patterns she was disposing of and one of them was *Istanbul*. Peggy decided right then that she would make this rug her next project.

Peggy found the rug a delight to hook because there were no parts of the design that were repeated. She sent the pattern to her workshop teacher, Nancy Blood, who did the color planning and came up with 16 different 8-value swatches. Peggy loves the dyeing process almost as much as the actual hooking so she had a lot of fun dyeing the wool and spot dyeing the rug's background. But as she hooked she found it difficult to hook the two birds and their mass of feathers. Peggy found that because there was not much definition in the 8-value swatches the feathers just seemed to melt into each other. Then she remembered a technique taught to her years ago where thread from a darker piece of wool can be hooked around each feather. "It's a process that sounds deadly, but in fact is easy and fast," says Peggy. "One hooks in existing holes and not in every one, giving the illusion of an edge without it becoming a definite outline."

Peggy's *Istanbul* was an award-winner at the Gallery Show for the Pennsylvania Designer Craftsmen last November including Best in Show and Excellence in Craftsmanship. The colorful rug is now brightening Peggy's family room, along with many of her acquisitions from decades of travel and living in the Middle East. Another bit of proof that Peggy was meant to hook this rug was her chance meeting with the friend who originally sent Pearl McGown the card that inspired *Istanbul*. "She still had one of the cards and has provided me with a color copy of the original," Peggy remarks. "Now, one of my students is planning to hook the original colors. I can't wait to help work on the dyeing for this one!"

PEGGY HANNUM

LANCASTER, PENNSYLVANIA

After 27 years of teaching high school English, Peggy is now retired and has enjoyed a second career teaching rug hooking to over 40 students from her home studio. While she loves hooking rugs, it's dyeing and playing with color that she calls her "passions." She prefers fine shading using #3 and #4 cuts and has completed about 25 rugs, pictorials and many smaller pieces. Peggy is the recipient of numerous awards in the fiber art and credits rug hooking teachers, Meredith LeBeau and Nancy Blood, for her more than 25 years of success. This marks Peggy's fifth appearance in A Celebration of Hand-Hooked Rugs. (See Peggy's beautiful Lancaster County home decorated with many of these rugs on page 84.)

Istanbul, 60" round, #3 and 4-cut wool on linen, 2003. Designed by Pearl K. McGown

In the Judges' Words

"GOOD CONTROL OF COLORS. SHOWS
MOVEMENT WITHOUT BEING BUSY."

"INCREDIBLY RICH AND COMPLICATED
COLOR SCHEME—BALANCE IS A
SUBTLE GREEN."

Little Mabel

The photograph of a little girl hoping for a catch at a country creek reveals a time of simple pleasures and carefree days. But for Laura W. Pierce, it is an endearing image of her three-year old grandmother photographed by her great grandmother on September 15, 1890. Laura never met her grandmother but knew she wanted to bring out the photograph's qualities and sweet memories through fiber art.

Laura began planning her rug two years ago at an Elizabeth Black workshop sponsored by her Association of Traditional Hooking Artists guild. At first, Laura wanted to hook the entire photograph but Elizabeth suggested that she focus on the little girl and not so much on the backdrop. After thinking it over, Laura decided that Elizabeth's recommendation was a good one and got to work. She used Photoshop to crop the photo, enlarged it to match the rug's dimensions, and finally transferred it to her linen backing. Even though the photograph was taken before the era of color pictures, Laura wanted to bring the photo to life by adding color to the rug's design. "Using scans from color photos of my own daughter at three or four-years-old, I pulled color samples from her cheeks, lips and skin," recalls Laura. "Color photos of a creek in the Sierra Foothills gave me ideas for water colors."

Laura dyed skin tones, gathered various gray flannels and plaids for the rocks, some black, lots of greens, some sky blue and white, and a little flower color. This project was Laura's first experience using #3-cut wool and she discovered that she loved the detail that resulted. Surprisingly, Mabel's face and hair came together very quickly, and only a few pieces of skin colored wool were required, but Mabel's hands turned into "baseball gloves" when Laura began hooking them. "Accuracy is not required when representation can do the job, so three fingers were better than four in this situation," Laura explains.

The rocks served as another hurdle but Laura solved the dilemma by making frequent references to the photograph and using a brown tweed for the shadows. When she noticed that the background was becoming a blur, Laura filled it with various leftover greens and hid her signature in the foliage. To hook the water, she put in blue and white sky reflections, a few colors from the bank, then filled in the rest with blues and greens.

Little Mabel is now in Laura's family room and has established an unbroken connection between her and the grandmother she never knew.

LAURA W. PIERCE
PETALUMA, CALIFORNIA

Laura W. Pierce's mother started making rugs when she was pregnant with Laura and that passion for fiber art must have rubbed off. Laura has been hooking rugs since 1996 and is basically self-taught by quietly observing other guild members. "I learned the hard way," Laura remarks. "My early rugs are quite packed. Now I teach and I instruct my students to skip holes and have loops just touch." She has been designing her own patterns from the start and leans towards the whimsical, geometric, and memorial. Laura continues to be challenged by the artistic play of color and texture in rug hooking and calls it "a forgivable art and a peaceful pastime."

In the Judges' Words

"I LIKE THE FOREGROUND."

"LOVELY FOLIAGE IN THE BACKGROUND. LINEAR WATER IS A NICE CONTRAST TO THE 'SOFT ROCKS.'"

Little Mabel, 15" x 20", #3 and 4-cut wool on linen, 2003. Adapted from a photograph.

Mottled Duck

Many rug hookers find it easier to use commercial patterns or their own designs when working on a project, but Jon Ciemiewicz was so intrigued by the original painting for the 2000 Federal Duck Stamp that he wanted to transform it into fiber art. He made several attempts to get permission from the painting's creator, Adam Grimm, who was reluctant at first because he had not seen any of Jon's work and did not want his picture done by someone who would not do it justice in a different media. Adam finally gave his stamp of approval and Jon was free to move forward with his rug project.

Although Jon loved the original painting, he wanted to incorporate several changes in his fiber adaptation. In the original, the water filled in all of the background and the duck's image was done in fairly bright sunlight. But Jon wanted to express his own creativity by having his rug reflect a sunset. To do that, Jon added a horizon line with hills and a setting sun behind the duck's head. Jon planned the duck's colors based on the original work of art but muted them more because of the sunset theme. He hand dyed all the wool utilizing various dyeing methods including dip, jar, and pot dyeing.

Jon's biggest challenge in hooking *Mottled Duck* was getting the sunset sky behind the duck without overpowering the image. He found that by putting the setting sun behind the duck's head, the bright sky was captured without detracting from the duck itself. Another challenge was finding wool material that could be overdyed and that would cut to a #3 to create the illusion of ripples in the water at the horizon line. "I enjoyed the total creation of this rug even though the background of the water and the sky provided a challenge," Jon remarks. "There was not a hum-drum aspect to the whole piece."

The water became Jon's favorite part of the rug because he believes it effectively reflects the sunset colors and gives depth to the rug by wave patterns that gradually decrease as they become more distant. Hooking the water in this way also taught him a better appreciation for how to incorporate depth-of-field into a rug.

Adam Grimm, needn't have worried about Jon's rendition of his original work of art. *Mottled Duck* has already won best of show at the Rochester State Fair. The rug is proudly displayed in an upstairs hallway inside Jon's home.

JON CIEMIEWICZ
LITCHFIELD, NEW HAMPSHIRE

Jon Ciemiewicz wanted to do some type of tactile craft after watching his wife working on knitting and crocheting projects. He tried cross-stitch and latch hook but they lacked something that traditional rug hooking offered. Seven years ago after a 15-minute lesson in the basic technique, Jon completed a square apple tile kit and has been hooking ever since. He has completed approximately 30 pieces and prefers hooking wildlife, primarily in a #3 cut in order to get the detail he desires. Jon has been teaching rug hooking for the past few years and this year is scheduled to teach at numerous rug schools throughout the northeastern United States and Canada.

In the Judges' Words

"THE DUCK AND WATER ARE BEAUTIFUL."

"GREAT LIGHT EFFECT. IT GLOWS!"

Mottled Duck, 24" x 30", #3-cut wool on polyester, 2003, Adapted from a stamp by Adam Grimm.

Please Do Not Feed the Artists

Since 1976, Carrie Jacobus has spent her summers teaching art and craft classes at Chautauqua Institution in Chautauqua, New York, an enclave where arts and culture are nurtured and nourished. It is a peaceful yet exciting locale where people go to get away from the hustle and bustle of their everyday lives and embrace their creativity. A photography book Carrie owned that depicted this artistic utopia inspired *Please Do Not Feed the Artists*. "When the winter weather gets me down, I open the book that sits on my living room table and I am immediately transported to the warm summer days in Chautauqua," Carrie says. "When I saw the photos of the art studios, I knew this would be the inspiration for my next rug hooking project. I also knew that I had accumulated wonderful brightly colored wool that was transition and spot dyed."

Carrie contacted the photographer who was intrigued by Carrie's request and gave her permission to transform some of the book's images into fiber art. Carrie drew a combination of two of the photographs from the book and transferred the pencil drawing onto monk's cloth. The strong values of the bright and lively wool colors proved to be a challenge but Carrie found that the piece just seemed to paint itself. Although she was not afraid to tackle a complicated or time-consuming project, she made the rug small for a reason. One of her main objectives was to finish the piece during her December break from school where she teaches chemistry—a scientific discipline that has strongly influenced the way Carrie observes, thinks, and creates. "Miraculously, the piece just flowed and five days of intensive and blissful hooking completed the picture," Carrie recalls.

Carrie says that the cohesive picture formed by two separate photographs she discovered in a much-loved book speaks to her artistic side and is a reminder of the place she keeps returning to time and time again. The rug is now displayed in Carrie's living room, and its presence is a spirited and colorful keepsake during those chilly winter days.

CARRIE JACOBUS

ORADELL, NEW JERSEY

A one-hour private lesson with a McGown certified instructor at Chautauqua Institution in 1996 was all it took to get Carrie Jacobus involved in the art of rug hooking. Since then she has tried many different rug hooking techniques, experimenting on her own, taking private lessons, and attending the Green Mountain Rug Hooking School. Carrie has received two commissions for fiber art—one to design a Jewish wedding canopy for a local temple, and the other a request for a banner from the Chautauqua Literary and Scientific Circle, the oldest continuous book club in the country. That banner is now part of a permanent collection in Alumni Hall at the Chautauqua Institution.

In the Judges' Words

"NICE USE OF COLOR!"

"FEELS LIKE AN ARTIST'S WATERCOLOR."

Please Do Not Feed the Artists, 12 ¹/₂" x 17 ¹/₂", #3 and 5-cut wool on monk's cloth, 2003.

Square Harmony

Connie Baar loves to surround herself with rich vibrant colors. Brilliant hues and the more exciting colors of the rainbow are not only apparent in her Tempe, Arizona home, decorated in red with mustard and olive accents, but also in her head where red seems to be her color of choice. *Square Harmony* comprised all the aspects of a rug that Connie loved—those exhilarating colors incorporated in a pattern containing both geometric and floral elements. "I chose this pattern for its variety of motifs," Connie says. "I prefer non-directional designs. I found this rug to be a lot of fun and it held my interest to the finish."

Connie began hooking *Square Harmony* in a workshop taught by Monika Jones and did the color planning using mostly over-dyed new wool in #8-cut with some #6-cut. While many rug hookers who dye their own wool follow a recipe to get the exact color they want, Connie relied on what she visualized in her head and her personal preferences, particularly using glorious red, a color that seems to appear in all of her hooking projects. What eased the process of hooking the rug's lively design was the fact that Connie had Monika's original rug to look at while she hooked even though both rugs were quite different in color and hooking style. Seeing how the other rug was hooked helped Connie in planning her winning entry and proved to be much easier than a line drawing.

One aspect of the rug that Connie is particularly proud of is not only its energetic feel but also the background where she was able to give it the look of uneven fading using as-is textures. Connie threw out the rulebook and relied on her imagination to hook some of the flowers and leaves in order to achieve primitive shading. It took Connie about six months to complete *Square Harmony*, finishing it off by folding the linen forward and then whip stitching it with thick wool yarn.

Connie's taste for color and design along with her attention to detail has served her well—*Celebration XIV* is the first competition she has ever entered. *Square Harmony* is now making beautiful music in Connie's kitchen, the perfect complement in color scheme and ambience to the home she loves.

CONNIE BAAR

TEMPE, ARIZONA

As far back as she can remember, Connie Baar has had art in her life, whether it be drawing, painting, or needle arts. Ten years ago, she took her first rug hooking class at a Phoenix quilt shop and now calls primitive rug hooking her exclusive creative outlet. "I found antique hooked rugs catching my eye in books and magazines," Connie says. "I was drawn to the naive quality of the designs." Along with the joy she gets from hooking commercial patterns and creating her own designs, Connie loves the fact that she has met so many wonderful and talented people through rug hooking.

In the Judges' Words

"SUBTLE WITH SPARKS OF RED. NICE PRIMITIVE."

"NICE VARIETY IN CENTER SQUARE MOTIFS."

Square Harmony, 32" x 52", #8-cut wool on linen, 2003. Designed by Monika Jones.

Turkish Primitive

Some rug hookers decide to hook a particular design because it conjures up a pleasant memory or it's a motif that will beautify a room in their home. Sue Hoss chose to hook *Turkish Primitive* for the sheer experience of hooking a big rug and creating its unusual pattern. In the past, she hooked dozens of smaller projects like mats and liked the instant accomplishment she felt from starting and completing something that was not large in size. From the onset, Sue knew that *Turkish Primitive* would prove to be a different sort of challenge.

Sue did the color planning and decided that blue was the primary shade she wanted in the rug. After finding an as-is blue wool for the background, she found that the rest of the colors naturally came and blended in just like she wanted. The rest of the wool was hand-dyed using an open dye pot method. The color combinations turned out to be Sue's favorite aspect of *Turkish Primitive*.

Sue found that she needed to pay close attention when she began hooking the swirls in the outer border squares because two different colors were used and directions changed. "I wanted an even flow to the curves and the corner squares provided pivotal points of direction," Sue explains.

When it came time for Sue to finish the rug, she used cording and whip stitched the edge with wool yarn. A cotton twill binding was then attached to the burlap backing along with a fringe.

Sue's determination paid off in completing her large rug project. She hooked the rug on and off for a year, many times putting it down and returning to those smaller pieces that always allowed her to see a finished result in a shorter amount of time. But once she completed the 32" x 56" *Turkish Primitive*, she learned that she could indeed hook a large rug and that finally seeing the completed project gave her a great deal of satisfaction. "There were days when I gave it my best and only finished a square," Sue says, "but I persevered and I'm happy to have completed it."

Sue plans on using this rug as a floor covering for her boys' room. It will always be a reminder of her first "big" accomplishment with her fiber artistry.

SUE HOSS

ROCKFORD, ILLINOIS

Five years ago, Sue Hoss saw a sample of a hooked rug at a local quilt shop, signed up for a two-hour class, and soon gave up her interest in other types of needlework arts. A year later she started Hoss-Town Cottage Classics where she provides the beginning rug hooker with options in simple patterns and kits. "One of my objectives as a rug hooker is to be accessible to beginners in my area and to keep up-to-date on rug hooking information," Sue says. Last year, Sue sent a mat she hooked to First Lady Laura Bush, which was received by the White House.

In the Judges' Words

"BEAUTIFUL COLOR COMBINATION."

"RICH, RICH COLORS AND EXPERT USE OF TEXTURES AND SOLIDS."

Turkish Primitive, 32" x 56", #7-cut wool on burlap, 2003. Designed by Jane McGown Flynn.

Winter Wonder

A themed exhibit titled "Fantasy Forest" announced by Mary B. Tycz's guild, Colonial Rug Hookers of Northern Virginia, was all the motivation Mary needed to create her rug *Winter Wonder*. Along with the topic, participants were given the drawing for a deciduous tree designed by another guild member. All other aspects of the depiction, including the bark, foliage, blossoms, fruit, setting, background, colors, technique, and materials were at the discretion of the fiber artist. Mary chose a cold night scene because, she says, "my personal thermostat is locked on high. I intended the rug to represent what I see in it—a refreshingly crisp moon-bright winter night luring me out for a walk to inhale its clean chilled air," Mary says. "Personal perspective is everything."

Winter Wonder turned out to be one of Mary's first pieces in many years and it taught her, among other things, that hooking is akin to creating a document on a computer and wanting to make it better.

She did a lot of reverse hooking in the four months she was working on the project, like when she tried to establish the contrast between the lines of the tree and the dark sky. She redid her first version that outlined the tree branches and trunk and replaced it with a shade lighter than the surrounding sky wool. She also discovered that the snow on the branches in front of the moon had to be very white while the snow on the branches set against the sky background had to be just a couple shades lighter than the night sky blues.

Mary's favorite part of creating the rug was hooking the moon. She found it interesting to hook a tight continuous-looking spiral that was broken up by the tree limbs, and varying the tinged blue-whites and wisps of magic light shooting out of it from the bottom left.

Even though *Winter Wonder* is finished, Mary still sees things that can be improved, particularly after looking at her close-up slides. "I learned to put the piece aside for a while, stand back, and take a good look before I reverse hook," she says. "A hooked rug truly exemplifies the expression, 'The whole is greater than the sum of its parts.'"

Mary has enjoyed the reactions of her non-hooking friends whose eyes light up when they first see *Winter Wonder*. "What they had interpreted as an exercise in domestic boredom is transformed into a piece of art that they seem to sincerely admire," Mary remarks.

MARY B. TYCZ

FALLS CHURCH, VIRGINIA

Mary Tycz grew up in a home surrounded by needlepoint, knitting, and wonderful rugs designed and hooked by her mother. While in college, Mary created a chair seat and small mat but waited 37 years until she hooked her third project—a fiber recreation of one of her mother's oil paintings. Although she also does cross stitch and embroidery, Mary has found rug hooking to be the most satisfying because it gives her a greater sense of freedom and creativity. A small mat she designed and hooked is currently part of a new traveling exhibit of mats created to be part of a children's alphabet book "Pieces of the World" that benefits the treatment of infants with clubfoot in developing countries.

Winter Wonder, 18 ¹/₂" x 17 ¹/₂", #3-6-cut wool on linen, 2003. Designed by Stacy LeCure and Mary Tycz.

In the Judges' Words

"I CAN FEEL THE COLD. NICE TREE
AGAINST THE FULL MOON."

"NICE MONOCHROMATIC."

SHOWCASE OF

Honorable Mentions

Review these pages carefully, then mark and mail the ballot inserted into this book to vote for the rugs you consider the best of the best. For more information on how these rugs were selected, and how the Readers'-Choice Contest is run, see page 1.

ANIMAL/BIRD RUGS

For Jilian, 26 ³/₄" x 36 ¹/₂", #3-
and 5-cut wool on burlap. Designed
and hooked by Suzanne Hamer,
Wasco, Illinois, 2002.

ANIMAL/BIRD RUGS

*On the First Day of Christmas
of Peace,* 17 ¹/₄"x 28 ¹/₂", #3-cut
wool on linen. Designed by Pearl K.
McGown and Jane McGown
Flynn. Hooked by Lynne Fowler,
Westover, Maryland, 2003.

ANIMAL/BIRD RUGS

Phoebe, 12" x 18", #3- and 5-cut
wool on warp cloth. Designed and
hooked by Anne E. Wickman,
Endicott, New York, 2003.

FLORAL/NATURE RUGS

Fairy's Cushions, 26" x 39", #3-5-cut wool on monk's cloth.
Designed by Pearl K. McGown. Hooked by Jean Coon,
Corona Del Mar, California, 2003.

FLORAL/NATURE RUGS

On Top of the World, 41" x 41", #6-cut wool on burlap.
Designed and hooked by Kath Kornelson Rutherford,
Musquodoboit Harbour, Nova Scotia, 2002.

FLORAL/NATURE RUGS

Sweet Sixteen, 11" x 43", #3-cut wool on cotton. Designed by
Jane McGown Flynn. Hooked by Sachiko Toyoda,
Kanagawa, Japan, 2003.

Gabbeh, 34 ¹/₂" x 53", #5- and 6-cut wool on linen. Designed by Jane McGown Flynn. Hooked by Cindy MacMillan, Newtown, Pennsylvania, 2003.

ORIENTAL/ETHNIC/GEOMETRIC/FOLK ART RUGS

Five Star One, 4' x 4', #4-cut wool on burlap. Designed and hooked by Nell Greenfieldboyce, Washington, D.C., 2003.

ORIENTAL/ETHNIC/GEOMETRIC/FOLK ART RUGS

Hanabi, 37" x 22", yarn on Scottish burlap. Designed by Toyokuni Utagawa. Hooked by Toshie Hayami, Tokyo, Japan, 2003.

ORIENTAL/ETHNIC/GEOMETRIC/FOLK ART RUGS

Here Comes Santa Claus Dummy Board, 20" x 48", #3-
and 4-cut wool on monk's cloth. Designed by Joan Moshimer.
Hooked by Kathryn Argauer, Kensington, Maryland, 2003.

PICTORIAL RUGS

Autumn at Lake Artemesia, 20" x 22 $^1/_4$", #3-cut wool on linen.
Designed and hooked by Bernice Howell, Beltsville, Maryland, 2003.

PICTORIAL RUGS

Eighteenth Century Fable,
11'7" x 8'3", #3-, 4- and 5-cut wool
on rug warp. Designed by Harry M.
Fraser. Hooked by Victoria Calu,
Dublin, Pennsylvania, 2003.

PICTORIAL RUGS

Homecoming at Fairfield Church, Circa 1940, 25" x 20", #3-cut wool on linen.
Designed and hooked by Sarah Lee Province, Silver Spring, Maryland, 2002.

PICTORIAL RUGS

Ivan's Village, 22 1/2" x 18 1/2", #3-cut wool on monk's cloth. Designed by Jane McGown
Flynn. Hooked by Lee Anne Aldred, Nashville, Tennessee, 2003.

PICTORIAL RUGS

Me and My Chicken, 24″ x 44″, #3-, 4-, 6- and 8-cut wool
on monk's cloth. Designed and hooked by Sandra Marquis,
Wallingford, Vermont, 2002.

PICTORIAL RUGS

My Favorite Lighthouses, 30 ¹/₂″ x 5′3″, #6- and 8-cut wool
on monk's cloth. Designed and hooked by Lucinda Pratt,
Excelsior, Minnesota, 2003.

PICTORIAL RUGS

Old Key West, 50 ¹/₂″ x 25″,
#3-cut wool on linen. Designed
and hooked by John Flournoy,
Millsboro, Delaware, 2003.

PICTORIAL RUGS

Sentinels, 26″ x 13″, *hand cut wool and other fabrics on linen. Designed and hooked by Mary Jane Andreozzi, Seekonk, Massachusetts, 2003.*

PHOTOGRAPHY BY PETER BARSS, BRIDGEWATER, NOVA SCOTIA

PRIMITIVE/WIDE-CUT RUGS

Big Flowers, 60″ x 66″, ¹/₂″ *ripped strips of wool on polyester. Designed and hooked by Wendy Richardson, Bridgewater, Nova Scotia, 2003.*

PRIMITIVE/WIDE-CUT RUGS

Commissioned Kitchen Rug, 60″ x 67″, *#6- and 8-cut wool on monk's cloth. Designed by Jane Olson. Hooked by Lynne Howard, Calgary, Alberta, 2003.*

Poppy, 35" x 34", #4- and 7-cut wool on linen. Designed and hooked by Judy Fresk, Glastonbury, Connecticut, 2003.

PRIMITIVE/WIDE-CUT RUGS

Retro Rocket, 26" x 38 ¹/₂", #7-cut wool on monk's cloth.
Designed and hooked by Roberta Burnes,
Lexington, Kentucky, 2003.

PRIMITIVE/WIDE-CUT RUGS

Pricilla Primitive, 58" x 32", #6-cut and hand-cut wool on linen. Designed by Ralph Burnham.
Hooked by Nancy Z. Parcels, Mechanicsburg, Pennsylvania, 2004.

SHOWCASE OF

Original Designs

Review these pages carefully, then mark and mail the ballot inserted into this book to vote for the rugs you consider the best of the best. For more information on how these rugs were selected, and how the Readers'-Choice Contest is run, see page 1.

Calypso

It took the worst ice storm in history and being homebound to spur Melissa Elliott to begin hooking her colorful *Calypso*. "I had just recently designed a rug pattern that I was particularly fond of," she recalls. "All my friends loved it and I had sold several. I planned to hook it one day but knew instantly that that day was here."

With the weather gray and dismal outside, Melissa knew she wanted to use bright colors in her rug. The only problem was what to use for the background. She wanted to avoid using solid black because she feared that the contrast would be too stark against the turquoise, apple green, purple, and orange. Melissa tried dyeing three yards of wool but decided to use all of her test batch wool for the rug instead of her final formula. The result was a much more interesting background especially when she added strips of an orange spot she had dyed and originally thought she wouldn't use. "Those random strips gave the flowers movement and so I named the rug *Calypso*—after a colorful Mexican dance," she explains.

Melissa knew where every color was going and hooked about a third of the rug in a two-week period. The big bold areas of color hooked quickly and easily in a #8 cut but the biggest challenge for Melissa was the basket. From the beginning that part of the rug was on her mind and Melissa avoided hooking it until the end, hoping for a brainstorm that would tell her what the basket should look like. "I finally decided that it didn't have to look like a basket as it was a primitive after all," she says, "so I just relaxed and hooked it like a child might color it, which was the way the rest of the rug had been hooked anyway!"

Besides creating the actual design for the rug, Melissa's favorite part of hooking is the finishing. Tidy edges are important to her and it's one of the things she looks for in any rug. For *Calypso*, she dyed her yarn, whipped the edge and then finished the back edge with rug tape. "Everyone thinks I'm crazy but I can't wait to get the binding and rug tape on," she says.

Since finishing the rug, Melissa hasn't decided where to display *Calypso*. She thinks it may end up on a wall in her children's television room. But no matter where its resting place, its vivid colors and happy essence will dispel those dreary winter days.

MELISSA ELLIOTT

VERSAILLES, KENTUCKY

Melissa Elliott was introduced to hooked rugs by her grandmother and, after taking one class, knew she had discovered her creative niche. In the fall of 2002, Melissa wanted to share her passion and organized the Heart of the Bluegrass Hookers, now 15 members strong. The group is in the process of becoming a member of the Association of Traditional Hooking Artists—the first in Kentucky. "I truly believe that God has answered my prayers by giving me the talent and enthusiasm that I have for my rug hooking," says Melissa, "and that somehow, He will use me to guide others to Him while inspiring them to hook along the way!"

In the Judges' Words

"HAPPY—JOYOUS USE OF COLOR!"

"GREAT USE OF PRIMARY AND SECONDARY COLORS."

"DANCE OF COLOR IS A GOOD MATCH TO THE DESIGN—NICE ENERGY."

Calypso, 28" x 49", #8 and 9-cut wool on linen, 2003.

Crewel World

Kris Noble's love of crewel-type designs, fantastical flowers and leaves, and unique colorful blooms led her to hook *Crewel World*. Although she had designed several other crewel patterns, this was the first one she did which had plants as the main part of the motif.

Kris, excited about the multi-color palette this rug would require, did her own color planning, and sketched a colored pencil drawing of *Crewel World* before beginning to hook. She worked backwards from her stash instead of dyeing to plan, since she exclusively uses over dyed, recycled wool instead of "as is," and experimented with a variety of dyeing techniques. "I dye 'by gosh and by golly' and find that crewel designs are a great place to utilize all those bits and pieces," Kris explains. "I don't have to worry about running out of anything."

Although Kris had a good idea of what she wanted color-wise, she still experienced a rocky start when she began hooking. Two days into the project, she decided that she didn't have the values she needed to create enough contrast because her stash tends to be short on light and bright swatches and long on darker, duller ones. "After a week of stewing, I ripped everything out, rethought the contrast problem, and took the opportunity to rework part of the design," Kris recalls. "When I started over, extensive use of complements and near-complements helped to provide the necessary 'pop.'"

Because of the diversity of flowers and plants in the rug's design, Kris discovered that creating cohesion and achieving an overall color balance and consistent level of contrast were the bumps in the road as her project progressed. To tie the motifs together, Kris intentionally spread some of the color from one plant to other areas to obtain the unity she wanted. *Crewel World* also forced Kris to relearn about contrast, its importance to the look and texture of the rug's motif, and to not fear the end result. It was a reminder that she needed to get out of her comfort zone and make bolder color choices. She ended up having fun hooking the rug because of the various motifs.

Kris developed each of the six plants in a square and arranged them in a quilt-like set with corner blocks placed on the diagonal. To finish it off, she whipped yarn around the corded edge and applied rug tape to the back of the primitive burlap.

KRIS NOBLE

VANCOUVER, BRITISH COLUMBIA

Before marrying and moving to Canada in 1987, Kris Noble worked in the menswear fabric design department at Pendleton Woolen Mills as a fabric stylist. At the time she didn't know about rug hooking but five years ago she began reading everything available with an eye toward weaving rugs. Soon thereafter, she happened upon a small box of colorful hand-dyed wool packed with accessories and immediately began hooking. "When I hook a little of Pendleton's wool into each rug, I always get a special sense of the creative continuity in my life," remarks Kris. This self-taught rug hooker has discovered that she loves the craft because of its flexibility and creative risk-taking.

In the Judges' Words

"THE COLOR BOUNCING OFF THE BLACK BACKGROUND IS WONDERFUL—LIGHT, BRIGHT, DARK, AND DULL."

"NICE COLOR HARMONY."

"GREAT COLOR CONTRASTS. IT MOVES!"

Crewel World, 35 1/2" x 48 1/2", #6-cut cool on burlap, 2003.

Dance of Life

Dance of Life conjures up some bittersweet memories for Cecille Caswell. She began the colorful and lively work of art at a fun-filled rug retreat in the mountains of Alberta, Canada, following the tragic loss of her first hooking teacher/mother-in-law, Shirley. That loss was coupled with the fact that Cecille was experiencing her own health issues. "I realized that I wanted to depict my love of life in a way that also depicts me," says Cecille. "I loved working on this piece. Missing my loved ones became less painful as each bright and colorful string was applied. Even the challenging moments were minimized as I kept in my mind "Live your life and forget your age.'"

Cecille's passion for bright colors and anything funky and non-traditional is embodied in this rug that made her happy and minimized her painful loss while she was working on it. She thought the project would be a simple and easy one but quickly discovered that it was not without its challenges and ended up making changes as she progressed to get the best result. Initially, she included ribbon and textured yarn as decoration but soon realized that they "jumped out" too much and became more of a distraction than an embellishment. She ripped them out and instead used wool for the self-expression she sought. Cecille also wanted her "lady" to appear to "glow." To achieve that effect, Cecille set white wool in a shallow pan with a small amount of water and painted from blue to yellow with the back of a spoon. She also learned the important lesson of always dyeing more than you need when she ran out of the blue/green "glow" and had to re-dye. Spot

and casserole dyeing enlivened the blues and purples and Cecille hooked in red and oranges to depict that explosion of energy from her exuberant dancing figure. The multi-colored whipped edge became the perfect finishing touch that tied the entire design together.

Cecille wanted this fiber creation to exude energy and a zest for life. With its creativity and color, Dance of Life has certainly accomplished that. The rug's design may be unconventional, but certainly not "off-the-wall" considering where it's presently displayed. "It was thrown over the back of a couch in my family room until I had my husband attach carpet nails to a board," Cecille remarks. "It is now hanging on the wall."

CECILLE CASWELL
ALBERTA, CANADA

For many years, Cecille Caswell would watch her mother-in-law, Shirley, hook beautiful rugs but the bug didn't bite Cecille until much later in 1988. Not only did Shirley pass on to her daughter-in-law a passion for the craft but also a love of bright colors. As a result, Cecille is very involved in the dyeing process in her attempt to create the brightest and most varied colors possible. Despite some of Cecille's vivid designs, she prefers the fine cut, more traditional pieces as a method to perfect her techniques. Cecille has received several first place finishes in the Alberta Foundation for the Arts, Focus on Fibre competition, as well as awards at the Edmonton Exhibition and the Fultonvale Country Fair.

In the Judges' Words

"MAKES ME FEEL LIKE A KID AGAIN!"

"NICE BALANCE OF VIBRANT COLORS. A FUN PIECE; NEAT WORK."

"WONDERFUL RICH COLORS AND BEAUTIFUL WOOL—EXUBERANT GREEN "AURA" IS A NICE TOUCH."

Dance of Life, 24" x 30", #4 and 5-cut wool on burlap, 2003.

Ethan and Friends

Louise Stancliffe calls it the "grandchildren series"—an array of individual wall hangings that pay tribute to each of her children's children. She had already completed rug projects that featured her daughters' children but needed one more that would feature her son's child, Ethan, Louise's youngest grandchild. The small blond-haired boy, two dogs, and a rural view of Iowa's farm fields were based on a selection of photographs that Louise used as a guide to create *Ethan and Friends*. "I've always enjoyed hooking the grandchildren and thinking about them as I hook," says Louise.

But working from the photos she had picked was no easy task. Louise discovered that the colors in the pictures did not seem "true" for either the foreground or the farm fields. She ended up taking many country drives so she could study the landscape and snap her own photographs of soy bean and alfalfa fields. Louise then examined those photos before she decided how to hook the open vistas depicted in her rug and what shades would work best.

Louise used mainly as-is wool from recycled materials or leftovers from other hooking projects. In most instances, gradation dyeing was used for the main subjects and spot dyeing for the farm fields and some of the foreground. She found that a piece of Dorr herringbone check was perfect for one of the fields and assorted greens that she had on hand from other projects worked beautifully for the trees appearing in the background.

This project was also the first time Louise ever hooked animals, but she looked forward to the challenge. Her attitude had always been that every rug is a learning experience and that each one requires special treatment. "The dog's fur was something I had not done before, and I found it required shading so the dogs were distinguishable," Louise says. "I found they were fun to do and I was pleased with the result. I am also happy that I was able to capture the feeling of distance across the fields."

Ethan and Friends marks Louise's second appearance in *A Celebration of Hand-Hooked Rugs*. The rug is now displayed on the dining room wall in the home of Louise's son and daughter-in-law.

LOUISE STANCLIFFE

ROCKFORD, ILLINOIS

Louise Stancliffe grew up watching her mother hooking rugs on old potato sacks and helped her search for wool fabric at rummage sales. It wasn't until many years later that Louise sought out a teacher to instruct her on the fine art of rug hooking. She now does her own dyeing and enjoys developing her own designs. Louise is currently working on a rug that will incorporate the various houses that she and her husband have lived in throughout their marriage as well as feature some of the events in their lives. Louise belongs to a small group of rug hookers in Northern Illinois and Southern Wisconsin who get together to hook and learn from each other.

In the Judges' Words

THE AGE OF INNOCENCE AND EXPLORATION SHINES THROUGH HERE. AND HIS TRUSTED FRIENDS WILL KEEP HIM SAFE."

"THE SOFT TRANQUIL COLORS GO WELL WITH THE PATIENCE THE DOGS ARE SHOWING."

Ethan and Friends, 30 ¹/₂" x 21", #3-5-cut wool on burlap, 2003.

Joy Ride

Peggy Northrop always liked silly, colorful things and leaned towards the whimsical in her fiber artistry. So when she traveled to the Cambria Pines Rug Camp, (Cambria, California) carrying a suitcase filled with #6 cut wool, she had the idea of creating a landscape fantasy rug representing the hills around her California home. She also wanted to depict a frog loosely based on the imported wooden frogs from Bali and Indonesia. But as Peggy began work on the rug, her teacher advised her to replace the #6 cut for #3 and #4 and do fine shading instead of the blocky colors Peggy had in mind.

Upon her return home, Peggy put aside the project for awhile. When she picked it up again, she sorted through her wool stash and pulled out all the colors that appealed to her and that seemed to go with any other color, and any plaid or texture that she liked. "By this time, my goal was to have fields in anything but green and to use as many textures and colors as I could," she says. "I'd also

read an article about hooking plaids while retaining their pattern and decided that was also a must for this rug."

Peggy laid out the plaids, textures, dyed, recycled, and new wool on a card table and sorted them into darks going up the sides, lights in the middle, and mediums all around. Starting in the lower right field, Peggy counted 17 different fabrics and realized that she better start keeping a log of all the fabrics and where they were used. She ended up incorporating a total of 207 different pieces of wool for the rug from as-is to tweeds. "Each afternoon I'd pull out the card table, review the remaining fabrics and the hooking so far, make changes as necessary, and begin hooking," Peggy says. "I'd take a digital picture every other morning or so, just to get a different perspective, and also made extensive use of my reducing glass. The hardest fields to do were the three small ones in the upper left as they were last to be hooked and I couldn't get the color/perspective just right."

Another challenge for Peggy was the sky because she wanted to use plaid but found it to be too much for around the frog. Her solution was to create a cloudy green sky by boiling down and over dyeing some of the plaid.

Joy Ride won best of show at the Sonoma County Fair last year. The rug is presently taking flight in Peggy's kitchen whose walls are being repainted in cantaloupe and lemon yellow to match this "can't help but make you smile" work of art.

PEGGY NORTHROP

SEBASTOPAL, CALIFORNIA

Peggy Northrop, who learned to sew at age seven, recalls being "totally drawn" to a rug hooking demonstration and fascinated by the wonderful color palette of wools she observed at a local county fair. Several years later, she came across a rug hooking brochure, found a teacher, took a half-day class and started hooking. Her enjoyment of rug hooking has replaced her past hobbies of needlepoint, teddy bear-making, and creating reproduction antique doll clothing. She mostly designs her own patterns and has tried just about every aspect of hooking-from fine to wide cut, shaded to primitive. Peggy is vice-president of the Wine Country Rug Hookers, a group affiliated with the Association of Traditional Hooking Artists.

Joy Ride, 30" x 27", #3-6-cut wool on linen, 2003.

In the Judges' Words

"WHIMSICAL! GREAT USE OF PLAIDS TO SHOW OFF
THE FIELDS."

"GREAT! I LOVE THE PLAID SKY, AND THE FROG
AND THE WAY THE LANDSCAPE PICKS UP
THE FROG'S CLOTH."

"WHAT A FROG! LOVE THE GROUNDWORK PATTERNS
AND COLORS. LOVE THE PLAID SKY!"

Nauset Lighthouse

Over the years, Patti Varley's family enjoyed vacationing on Cape Cod, especially at Eastham where the Nauset Lighthouse was located along the seashore. She recalled looking up at the lighthouse from the beach below and envisioned herself in the keeper's house and imagined what it would be like to live there. It always remained a kind of mystical place that she would think about even during the daily routines of her day. Recreating that beautiful memory into fiber art became a type of meant-to-be opportunity when Patti signed up for a class in family heirlooms at the Green Mountain Rug School.

Patti segued easily into transforming the New England vacation spot into fiber art. She adapted the pattern from one of her photographs using a light projector and transferred it to a linen backing. When it came time to do the color planning, Patti simply followed the natural colors found in the picture. Wool for the sand was spot dyed to obtain the look of shifting dunes and she had swatches gradation dyed for the lighthouse, keeper's house, cottage, and sky. Patti took pleasure in hooking the lighthouse and loved watching how it soared above the cliff as each piece of wool was looped into the linen backing. But Patti admits that the sky presented her with the biggest challenge because she had difficulty finding just the right values of blue. "After several reverse hooking sessions, Rose Korb, my teacher at the Easton Rug Hooking Group suggested the formula for the sky," Patti recalls. "After dyeing it using an open pan eye-balling method, I was delighted with the effect."

Patti learned some important lessons from hooking *Nauset Lighthouse*. This rug project allowed her to step outside her comfort zone where she was accustomed to hooking mainly with wide cuts with little, if any, shade variations. As a result, she loved the realistic outcome she achieved—a result that mirrored the much adored vacation photograph she used as her guide. "It was a bit scary," Patti admits, "but the exploration of new techniques was gratifying."

Nauset Lighthouse is now framed and displayed in Patti's living room where, she claims, she "can almost feel the ocean breeze." But one of her most profound rewards from completing her fiber work of art is knowing that *Nauset Lighthouse* evolved from a beautiful scene in a photograph to a finished heirloom that her family would enjoy for years to come.

PATTI VARLEY
SARATOGA SPRINGS, NEW YORK

Patti Varley always admired and appreciated her mother's hooked rugs in the 1970s and 1980s but didn't start hooking on her own until 1996 when she joined a small rug hooking group in Easton, New York. Several years later, her rug hooking teacher, Dick LaBarge, asked Patti if she would be interested in helping him dye wool. Together, they self-published the dye book Dyeing from the Doo Dye Inn—Antique Primitive Colors *and co-authored the* Doo Dye Box Formulae. *Patti, formerly a nurse, belongs to the Green Mountain Rug Hooking Guild and the National Guild of Pearl K. McGown Rug Hookrafters.*

Nauset Lighthouse, 16 1/2" x 19 1/2", #3-cut wool on linen, 2002.

In the Judges' Words

"BEAUTIFUL—PEACEFUL AND A
PERFECT DAY TO SIT AND RELAX.
LOVE THE SKY—NOT A CLOUD."

"THE PICTURE IS VERY
WELL DONE."

"BEAUTIFUL GREENERY."

Night Mare

Karen Maddox didn't have to use a ready-made pattern or a photograph as a guide to hook *Night Mare*. Instead she used an oil painting that she created herself to transform an image from canvas to linen. "I thought the colors would be interesting to try to simulate in wool," says Karen. "The title refers to a mare at night. Hence, I could experiment with some different colors."

As a painter of oils and pastels, Karen was used to squeezing colors out of tubes, mixing them with ease to obtain the shade she desired, and then simply brushing them onto a canvas. But with rug hooking, Karen discovered that it was much harder to paint with wool. Using her painting of the horse as a reference to color plan her rug project, Karen hooked the horse's muzzle, nostril, eyes, ears, and the light side of the face from her scrap bag of leftover wool. The mane, light side of the neck, and light border area were dip dyed, and the dark areas of the neck and background were hooked from as-is wool from skirts and slacks that she had collected from thrift shops. The dark background and dark areas of the horse were Karen's favorite parts to hook because she loved using the skirts and slacks to insert the texture the material provided. "My favorite part of the rug is the horse's face, as she seems to want to be stroked," says Karen.

One of the most challenging aspects of the rug for Karen was the nostril because it kept growing larger as she hooked and she was forced to take out several rows before it "fit." The solution was to stay on the inside of the outline rather than hook right on it. Hooking the background proved to be another formidable task for her because she had to intersperse several fabric colors to keep it interesting without taking away from the horse. Karen whipped the edges with wool yarn—two navy strands plus one maroon strand—to simulate the colors of the background. She then hand-stitched it with rug tape.

Night Mare is Karen's third rug to appear in *A Celebration of Hand-Hooked Rugs*. The rug is now hanging in Karen's living/dining room area.

KAREN MADDOX

KERRVILLE, TEXAS

Karen Maddox's introduction to rug hooking happened while browsing the magazine rack at the bookstore. She began flipping through Rug Hooking *magazine and was drawn to the colors and textures shown on its pages. "I bought the edition and found that it was possible to do your own designs," Karen explains. "This really interested me, as I have always wanted to find a needlecraft where I could do my own thing." She calls her first project a lesson in "what not to do." Karen has now been creating fiber art for more than five years and has completed about 10 rugs and wall hangings, plus smaller items such as pillows, doorstops, and Christmas ornaments.*

In the Judges' Words

"GORGEOUS HORSE. THE EYE STARES RIGHT AT YOU."

"GREAT USE OF COLOR FOR THE HORSE."

"GOOD USE OF LIGHT SOURCE. SHADING IS GREAT."

Night Mare, *21" x 27", #4-cut wool on linen, 2003.*

Oak Tree Longing

Sometimes inspiration comes from missing something so much that you just have to hook it into a rug in order to hold onto the memory. Such was the case with Linda Brown who began gathering pieces of wool that conjured up the rich hues of fall leaves, a reminder of the pastures and old oak trees she had left behind when she moved from a rural area to a new subdivision about four years ago.

Linda decided to turn her stack of wool into a rug of her own creation. She found the encouragement she needed to complete the design for *Oak Tree Longing* when she enrolled in a Pris Butler workshop. With Pris spurring her on, Linda drew a single square of her idea, made copies, and grouped them on the floor to determine the final arrangement. From there, the acorns and geometric squares evolved naturally into the final drawing. Linda's biggest challenge was not the actual hooking of the rug but the drawing of the design onto the monk's cloth. "In order to have perfectly straight lines that met properly at the corners, I had to count lines and draw carefully on the diagonal," recalls Linda.

Linda used leftover blackish background fabrics in various hues from green-black to plain black for around the leaves, and dark gold spot-dyed wool with tinges of red and green to delineate the squares and outline the rug. One of the things she learned while working on *Oak Tree Longing* was that the extra time spent on the rug's planning and design resulted in an easier hooking experience. During the 15 months it took to complete the rug, Linda took pleasure in seeing each leaf develop as the various textures, plaids, and tweeds were mixed. She developed a sense of satisfaction in

completing the 47" x 70" rug but, while doing so, worked on several smaller pieces as diversions to keep from feeling bogged down.

Miles away and years ago, Linda used to gaze at the stately old oak trees from the window of her former country home. Now her rug has become as vivid a memory to her as any photograph or realistic oil painting. *Oak Tree Longing* now warms the floor of her new family room in front of an old oak-framed Arts and Crafts sofa. "The two seem made for each other," Linda muses, "and I can once again see oak leaves any day."

LINDA BROWN
OVERLAND PARK, KANSAS

Linda Brown calls it "luck" when she made a quick stop to get calico for a crocheted rag rug about 10 years ago and happened upon Emma Lou Lais teaching rug hooking in the shop's classroom. Linda soon began taking classes and since then has hooked 15 rugs and 10 small pieces. Her early projects were hooked with #8 cuts in primitive style, but while designing a rug depicting the site of her oldest daughter's wedding, she learned to use any cut necessary to achieve the required detail. Linda has hooked both originals and commercial patterns but says her greatest feeling of accomplishment comes from completing a rug that is hers from start to finish.

In the Judges' Words

"NICE RUG. GOOD CONTRAST AND USE OF MULTIPLE COLORS IN THE LEAVES AND BACKGROUND."

"THE CRISP LINES AND DESIGN LAYERING IS VERY PLEASING."

"GREAT COMBINATION OF STRUCTURE (THE GEOMETRIC ELEMENT) AND THE NATURAL/ORGANIC (USE OF COLOR AND TREATMENT OF LEAVES)."

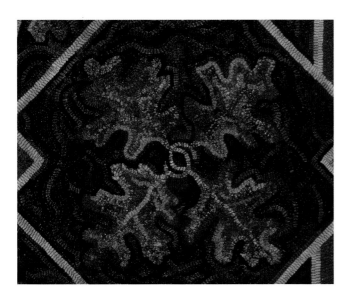

Oak Tree Longing, 47" x 70", #5-8-cut wool on monk's cloth, 2003.

Polo Play

Abby Vakay finds that fiber art allows her to pursue design and gives her a sense of satisfaction in completing a solid composition. But as she created her lively and active piece, *Polo Play*, she discovered that it allowed memories to resurface of sitting and enjoying this fascinating equine sport and of her time spent with horses while living in Pennsylvania, Virginia, and on Long Island, New York. This piece made of hand-dyed cut wool on linen backing had her reliving and savoring those glorious remembrances.

Abby started hooking *Polo Play* in the month of August, the height of the polo season on Long Island, and worked through the holidays to complete the project in January. She began by hooking the pony and rider in closest pursuit of the ball, then moved around the piece blending colors. Abby dyed all her own materials for the rug and had a general idea of what types of tones she wanted to bring out certain design aspects. She didn't preplan her palette but instead thrived on the fact that her color picks changed as she hooked. "My color plan was to work in very saturated hues," Abby explains, "with transcolored wools to show intense, hot highlights, and very shadowy cool lowlights, especially on the polo ponies."

Abby didn't allow the design to take control and dictate how it should turn out. Instead, Abby took artistic license in several areas. First, she replaced the icon on the tent that advertised a famous car dealer and instead used a peace sign—a symbol that she felt was fitting in today's world. Second, she wanted to place the sunset in view so she could play with the purples and oranges and, in the process, learned that less representational work could result in a better piece of art. In actuality, the sunset would have been behind her where she sits to watch the real thing on those August days in New York.

Abby admitted that her least favorite part of *Polo Play* was the sitting and pulling loops but instead of viewing it as a chore, she found it relaxing and soothing for the mind. "The tactile satisfaction of the fiber keeps me grounded as I work through to completion in a meditative way, day in and then day out."

Last summer, *Polo Play* graced the cover of *Dan's Papers*, a publication distributed throughout the Hamptons and the New York metropolitan area. The piece was also included in an article in *Rug Hooking* magazine, and was invited to appear in various shows around the United States.

ABBY VAKAY

ALEXANDRIA, VIRGINIA

Abby Vakay began hooking in 1991 under the guidance and support of her mentor, Mary Sheppard Burton. Abby has created a variety of hookings and loves the fact that her final images are always a surprise and quite different from anything she had planned. "As I continue exploring other ways to express myself in fiber, I seem to transcend my traditional boundaries and learn from the results," she says. Abby teaches yoga and rug hooking to inspire creativity and personal expression throughout the United States and Canada, at the Smithsonian Institution, the Springwater Fiber Workshop, and in her home studio.

In the Judges' Words

"THE NOISE AND EXCITEMENT CAN BE HEARD AS YOU LOOK AT THE MOTION SHOWN IN THESE HORSES."

"THERE IS A LOT OF COLOR USED TO INDICATE MOVEMENT, BUT YET IT DOESN'T TAKE AWAY FROM WHAT YOU ARE SEEING."

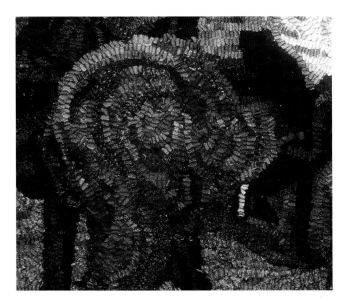

Polo Play, 20" x 29", #6-8-cut wool on linen, 2003.

Russian Birch

An art collector's request for a commissioned piece and her preference for birch trees became the impetus for Gene Shepherd to recreate the magical Russian landscape that he had traveled to in the past. It was a landscape that was seared into his mind, the sort of place, he says, where the "rigid lines of life intersect with a rich fantasy in art, music, and conversation."

Besides yearning to depict this magnificent country in fiber art, Gene had been looking for an excuse to experiment with cut size, color, and perspective. He knew he wanted to use strong geometric lines in a whimsical pastoral setting. He hooked very wide cuts in the forefront of the piece using vivid colors and then gradually decreased the size with a #3 and a couple of #2s in less intense shading to obtain that feeling of distance. "In one sense, it is a very structured piece," says Gene. "Rigid perspective lines clearly give it movement and direction. However, the perspective lines and outlines of the three main trees were the only pattern lines drawn. I wanted the hooking experience to be something like a walk in the forest—never knowing exactly what would come next—so I left my canvas blank."

Gene's client chose the colors since she wanted the piece to match her home. Gene employed almost every dye technique with no thought of exactly how the wool would be used. The birch wool was spot dyed over an assortment of cream, white, light plaids, and beige colored wool. "My challenge was to do the whole rug, in

bold perspective, with no printed design, using every cut with just the wool I had dyed," says Gene.

Gene found that he hooked in spurts and that ideas would come in a rush, allowing him to finish a section before inspiration would grind to a halt. During those times, Gene would hang *Russian Birch* in a place where he could study it while doing other things. Somehow ideas would start flowing again and Gene's work would resume. "I eventually got to the place where I didn't try to force hooking by schedule and only worked when I felt passionate about it," he explains. "I suspect that my visit to Moscow that fall was somewhat instrumental in determining the eventual feel of the piece."

When Gene completed the project and delivered it to his client's home, he was surprised to see that nearly every design element used in the rug's forest floor blended perfectly with the room's decor, details that were never before discussed with the client.

GENE SHEPHERD

ANAHEIM, CALIFORNIA

Gene Shepherd started hooking rugs on a whim when he decided that it was a way of taking a break from his weaving projects. Using craft store burlap, a crochet hook, hand cut wool, and his wife's quilt frames, he made his first rug in three weeks. Gene got so "hooked" that his love of weaving has been replaced by his passion for creating rugs. He is currently re-creating a second rug for the United States Department of Interior for the private office of Franklin Roosevelt at Hyde Park, New York. Gene is the director of the Cambria Pines Rug Camp and enjoys being the token male at many rug hooking gatherings.

In the Judges' Words

"I CAN FEEL THE DEPTH AND WANT TO WANDER THROUGH THE TREES."

"ABSTRACTION OF NATURAL ELEMENT IS WELL DONE."

Russian Birch, 29 1/2" x 66", #2-10-cut wool on monk's cloth, 2003.

Season's Cube Stool

Kim Nixon did not learn rug hooking in the traditional sense and so it is not surprising that her entry, *Season's Cube Stool*, be a multi-dimensional as well as a very functional work of art. "This design originated because of the four seasons matching the four-sided format of this stool," Kim explains. "Three-dimensionally, the stool unfolds calling the viewer to circle the stool to see the entire design. Each side had to be strong enough to stand on its own."

Kim was interested in creating a "twilight feel" for the piece and her fondness for green, related to green cheese moon folklore, made the moon the centerpiece and the top of the design. She hand-cut the wool as she worked, requiring that she pay attention to each strip hooked. Hooking in this manner allowed each of these strips to define the motif by adding to the volume for emphasis. One of Kim's challenges was the fact that the background was gradated in larger concentric circles moving outward from the moon on top. This added a difficulty factor to her pattern because darker and darker tones were worked in away from the moon down to the bottom edge. She did her own color planning and dyed textured and off-white wool from light greens to teal blue blacks to obtain the effect she wanted and created a swirling motion by interlocking colors. "I jokingly describe this as being rather like a toilet flushing and instantly my students know what I am talking about," says Kim. "Having the background show motion and not be static is one of my favorite parts of this design."

Because Kim's piece is a stool and not a wall hanging or floor covering, the finishing methods required a different type of expertise. *Season's Cube Stool* is on a padded wooden stool base with the bottom covered in a matching fabric. The legs are wormy oak, polished with a light Minwax. "Hooking this footstool brought me back to the kind of hooking I started with and has taught me to open my work up again to be more spontaneous. It is harder to not have it all completely figured out but the challenge keeps you more involved with each loop. I like that."

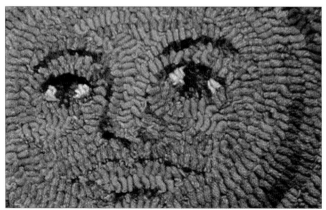

KIM NIXON

MARYVILLE, TENNESSEE

Kim Nixon's fondness for rug hooking began 13 years ago when she fell in love with the simple elegant primitive rugs she found in Jesse Turbayne's books on the history of rug making. Kim found that rug hooking not only complemented her fine art degree and her 25 years of experience as a painter, but the craft and its possibilities fueled her passion to create images in her own voice. "For this reason I just began, teaching myself from books, using what wool I could find and always designing my own patterns," says Kim who teaches footstool design at camps and workshops across the country. Since 2000, she has also run her own business, Under the Rug.

Season's Cube Stool, *13" x 13" x 16", hand-cut wool on linen, 2003.*

In the Judges' Words

"Beautifully done! Great use of color and design."

"Love the surface. It blends nicely down into the panels."

"Subtle use of textures."

The Morgan Rally Challenge

Lelia F. Ridgway believes that you should hook the things you like and one of her favorite things is her English sports car, a Morgan, and her memories of being a rally master for the Morgan sports car club rally. With that in mind, she decided to hook a whimsical story about a Morgan Rally. Her desire for detail resulted in her jumping into her car and driving the rally route located in Chester County, Pennsylvania. She snapped pictures along the way and, with photos in hand, planned some of the rally's highlights that she would incorporate in her rug.

Lelia immediately acknowledged some of the challenges that the project would present. How would she do the detail of the automobiles? How should she hook the animals? The answers came during a class Lelia attended about hooking with yarns and mixed fiber media. Lelia decided to appliqué the Morgans, using metallic embroidery thread for the chrome, and beads for the headlights with silver foil behind them. She even appliquéd a piece of glittery ribbon on the church for the window. Then the idea of needle felting all of the animals popped into her head. "Suddenly, I became possessed by this rug," Lelia says. "I could not stop working on it. Each car, animal, tree—everything became a part of my soul. I felted hair blowing in the wind, exhaust fumes from the cars, and smoke coming from the chimneys of the buildings. I felted the Amish farmer's mules. I had so much fun creating each vignette."

Along with the innovative applications she used in the project, like drawing clock faces for the racing officials' stop watches and gluing them onto little jewelry loops, Lelia also relied on rug hooking's more traditional techniques. She jar dyed some intense brilliant jewel tone rainbow colors for the cars and used a marbleized wool blended with some dip dyed blues for the creek. Lelia was so enthused about creating The Morgan Rally Challenge that she spent every spare second of her time working on it. After completing the 38" x 54" project in 54 days, Lelia felt like she had lost an "exciting friend." "I learned to combine all of my skills to create this rug," she says. "I used many of my embroidery techniques and appliqué skills from quilt making, plus I learned that you can felt right onto the foundation fabric."

The Morgan Rally Challenge is now a welcome friend inside Lelia's living room. "Each time I look at it," she remarks, "I remember the wonderful day running the rally and the exciting time I had hooking the story."

In the Judges' Words

"THE LIGHTER COLORS ARE USED WELL TO DRAW YOU INTO THE SCENE."

"INVENTIVE YET RESTRAINED. WELL BALANCED DESIGN AND COLOR. IT TELLS A STORY."

"CHARMING USE OF WOOL WITH MIXED MEDIA."

LELIA F. RIDGWAY
DOWNINGTOWN, PENNSYLVANIA

Lelia F. Ridgway recalls spending hours watching a rug hooker at a craft show in 1984 who recommended that Lelia subscribe to Rug Hooking magazine. Lelia took her advice and, upon receiving each issue, would drool over the exquisite rugs pictured on its pages saying to herself, "Some day I am going to learn this beautiful art form." After recovering from cancer in 1996, Lelia decided that "some day" had arrived. She signed up for hooking classes and, since then, has produced about six to ten rugs per year. Lelia has been the recipient of several awards for her fiber art including First Place People's Choice awards at the Brandywine Rug Hooking Guild and the Historical Yellow Springs Gallery of Excellence Show.

The Morgan Rally Challenge, 38" x 54", #3-, 4- and 8-cut wool, metallic threads and fleece on monk's cloth, 2003.

THE MORGAN RALLY CHALLENGE

The Parsonage on Star Island

Cosette Allen knew how to attract a crowd when she first began hooking *The Parsonage on Star Island*. Last summer, she was making plans to attend a weeklong church conference at this parsonage located off the New Hampshire coast and decided to begin hooking the rug that she had wanted to create for years. Before she left, she brought along a design she drew from photos she had taken in the past, a small suitcase of wool, and a desire to hook the parsonage's image onto synthetic linen backing. "I touched up the drawing while looking at the parsonage, and then I spent several hours that week sitting and hooking in a rocking chair on the porch of the hotel," she recalls. "Other people from the conference stopped by to see my progress and to see how it was done. "What a wonderful vacation." Cosette finished the rug at home a few months later in August of 2003.

What appears to be an unassuming little building surrounded by wild flowers speaks volumes for Cosette. Although there are other buildings on the island built from the same stone, this one is special, she says. It's a serene setting where tea is served every afternoon, and where iris, day lilies, and roses grow on their own with blossoms that almost cover the parsonage's entranceway. Cosette used mostly recycled wool in a #5 cut but used #3 and #4 for some of the finer parts of the flowers. The building itself was hooked from a piece of brown and gray plaid that she had been saving for years just for this project. From that plaid material, Cosette used the darker gray shade for the shadows. "I almost achieved my goal of making an entire rug without having to buy one single piece of wool, but I didn't make it," Cosette remarks. "To finish the rug I had to buy one piece of wool."

The biggest challenge for Cosette was hooking the rocks scattered on the cottage's lawn. She took them out several times until she was able to attain the multi-dimensional look she was after.

Cosette proudly displays *The Parsonage on Star Island* on a wall in her office and says it's almost like having an extra window.

COSETTE ALLEN

MONTPELIER, VERMONT

Cosette Allen began creating rugs 20 years ago when she and her husband traveled to Nova Scotia on vacation and visited a hooked rug museum. There, she watched a woman hooking and decided she wanted to learn. Once she returned home, she began taking classes from Sylvia Dole. Her first attempt, a combination floral and geometric design, was one she hated from the beginning. "It is a wonder that I ever finished it or continued to hook," she says. "I did learn how to shade and hook on that rug." Since then, Cosette has completed about 28 rugs and has won three awards including two rugs in the top ten People's Choices at the Hooked in the Mountains Rug Show at Shelburne Museum in Vermont.

The Parsonage on Star Island, *35" x 27", #3-5-cut wool on linen, 2003.*

In the Judges' Words

"LOVE IT!! WANT TO GO THERE.
COLOR, DESIGN AND EXECUTION
CALL ME TO COME."

"FACE OF THE COTTAGE LOOKS
WEATHERED AND OLD. IT GIVES A SOFT,
PEACEFUL EFFECT OVERALL."

"NICE SENSE OF ITS BEING REMOTE."

Welcome to the Barber Shop

You can't help but smile when you take a look at *Welcome to the Barber Shop*, a piece of fiber art filled with barbers' tools of the trade and four women ready and willing to do some makeovers. Kathy Baggett, a master barber by trade, began designing the rug when she and her three co-workers made plans to relocate their barbershop. In the midst of painting and decorating their new building, Kathy sought to create the type of rug that would not only become the shop's focal point but would also communicate a sense of celebration of the women's years of friendship and their new beginning. "I wanted it to project a rich and warm welcome to our customers, old and new," Kathy explains. "It was the blending of those goals, the skills I had learned, and a little whimsy thrown in for good measure, that resulted in the design creation."

It took five months for Kathy to complete *Welcome to the Barber Shop*—a rug that was not only fun for her to do but presented some new challenges such as outlining letters and hooking faces. She didn't attempt to create mirror images of her workmates pictured on the rug; instead, she sought a whimsical style for their likenesses. Except for the border and background, Kathy was able to use recycled wool that she already had on hand.

Welcome to the Barber Shop is proudly displayed in the women's shop and is drawing more attention than Kathy imagined. "What pleases me most is to hear the stories it inspires," she says. "Many of them start out, 'Who hooked that rug? My grandmother used to do that.' One man in his 80s brought in pictures of his mother hooking rugs. What a joy it was to hear his stories. They inspired me even more. Rug hooking truly is a legacy you can leave your family."

According to Kathy, the rug's quality and its playful portrayals have resulted in a few converts to the craft. Some of her customers have shown an interest in learning to hook and, in her never-ending quest to please her patrons, Kathy has put together several kits and gotten them started.

KATHY BAGGETT

HIXSON, TENNESSEE

Kathy Baggett always had a fascination with hooked rugs whenever she would pass by a decorating shop or spot them in a magazine. Twenty years ago, she went to a rug exhibit at the Chattanooga Trade Center where a family friend offered to teach her, but it took 12 more years before Kathy had the time to gather hooks, wool, and burlap and start creating fiber art. To date she has completed 42 rugs and purses. With the exception of two commercial patterns that she has purchased over the years, Kathy prefers designing her own and has won several ribbons for rugs entered in her local county fair exhibit, including a third place win for Welcome to the Barber Shop.

In the Judges' Words

"LOOKS LIKE A FUN SHOP. GREAT DESIGN. MAKES ME SMILE."

"FUN PIECE WITH NICE DETAILING."

Welcome to the Barber Shop, 60" x 35", #7-cut wool on linen, 2002.

Dear Celebration Reader:

YOUR VOICE MAKES A DIFFERENCE

Please extend your love and appreciation of the time and effort put into each hooked rug by giving your time to vote in the Readers' Choice Contest.

In an effort to expand our representation of the amazing diversity of this form of fiber artistry, **CELEBRATION XIV** includes five new honorable mention categories. In addition to the traditional voting of 1st, 2nd, and 3rd choice for the COMMERCIAL and ORIGINAL rug categories, please make your selection for the best of each of the five new HONORABLE MENTION categories: Animal/Bird Rugs, page 45; Floral/Nature Rugs, page 46; Oriental/Ethnic/Folk Art/Geometric Rugs, page 47; Pictorial Rugs, page 48; Primitive/Wide-Cut Rugs, page 51.

The time you take to send in your Readers' Choice vote is appreciated by us at *Rug Hooking* magazine and also by the rug hooking artists represented within the pages of **CELEBRATION XIV**.

Sincerely,

Ginny Stimmel

Ginny Stimmel
Editor

BUSINESS REPLY MAIL
FIRST-CLASS MAIL PERMIT NO. 1 LEMOYNE PA

POSTAGE WILL BE PAID BY ADDRESSEE

RUG HOOKING MAGAZINE
1300 MARKET STREET SUITE 202
LEMOYNE PA 17043-9945

NO POSTAGE
NECESSARY
IF MAILED
IN THE
UNITED STATES

BUSINESS REPLY MAIL
FIRST-CLASS MAIL PERMIT NO. 1 LEMOYNE PA

POSTAGE WILL BE PAID BY ADDRESSEE

RUG HOOKING MAGAZINE
1300 MARKET STREET SUITE 202
LEMOYNE PA 17043-9945

NO POSTAGE
NECESSARY
IF MAILED
IN THE
UNITED STATES

BUSINESS REPLY MAIL
FIRST-CLASS MAIL PERMIT NO. 1 LEMOYNE PA

POSTAGE WILL BE PAID BY ADDRESSEE

RUG HOOKING MAGAZINE
1300 MARKET STREET SUITE 202
LEMOYNE PA 17043-9945

NO POSTAGE
NECESSARY
IF MAILED
IN THE
UNITED STATES

When Mothers Can't Mother

Linda Friedman Schmidt's experiences being raised by a mother traumatized by the horrors of World War II and her social consciousness were the catalysts that impelled her to create *When Mothers Can't Mother*. For Linda it is a work of art that responds to the frightening world events of our time—to poverty, hunger, and war—all circumstances that prevent terrorized and distressed women from properly nurturing and nourishing their children. "The need for a nurturing mother, if unmet, has a profound impact on one's ability to function socially, as well as on one's basic biology," Linda explains. "Early emotional experiences influence us for the rest of our lives."

As a former fashion designer, Linda's fiber painting reflects her ease with color and fabric. She did not start out with a color plan but instead decided on each color as her project progressed. Because Linda has no formal art school education, she acknowledged that her biggest challenge was incorporating perspective and shading into her rug. Linda used her patience and observation skills to determine what looked right and what didn't. When something appeared off-kilter, she would simply do it over until it appealed to her senses.

When Mothers Can't Mother incorporates a variety of recycled fabrics. Besides wool, Linda also used silk, cotton, polyester, nylon, rayon, acetate, and combinations of all the above to represent transformation —old clothes into paintings, sadness into gladness.

But it is not only Linda's subject matter that made this work of art unique. Her finishing method, of hemming the edges before she begins to hook, is one she devised herself. "I sew thick canvas webbing all around the outside, leaving about 2" of backing all around," she explains. "I turn this 2" hem under and hook through it as I make my work. When I'm done, all you see is the neat webbing frame."

Linda's fascination with identity is depicted in the eyes and expressions of the five women and infant portrayed in *When Mothers Can't Mother*. The faces were Linda's favorite aspects of the fiber painting and she also learned how to deal with overlapping figures and the anatomy of the hands while hooking this piece.

When Mothers Can't Mother is presently on display at Seton Hall University gallery as part of an exhibition titled "Exploring Gender Roles." Linda is hopeful that her haunting fiber creation will motivate others to remedy the earth's ills. "It's an outcry for world peace in these profoundly disturbing times," she says. "Have we not learned from history?"

LINDA FRIEDMAN SCHMIDT
FRANKLIN LAKES, NEW JERSEY

Linda Friedman Schmidt's passion for fiber art began in 1998 when she came across the book Rag Rug Inspirations *in her local library. She taught herself to hook based on what appealed to her in the book, using one of her crochet hooks and a piece of burlap. "I never attended art school, never went to a camp or workshop," Linda says. "My credentials are my life experiences which surface in my work." As a teenager, Linda used to reconstruct old clothes into trendy styles and is accustomed to working with all types of fiber and fabric in her fiber paintings, even plastic bags if needed to illustrate an object or theme that she considers fake or unreal.*

In the Judges' Words

"THE EYES TELL THE WHOLE STORY. GREAT USE OF COLOR."

"WONDERFUL COLOR."

"POWERFUL MESSAGE."

When Mothers Can't Mother, 41" x 63", hand-cut strips of discarded clothing on cotton warp cloth, 2003.

Decorating with Hooked Rugs

A WALK THROUGH THE HOME OF MARGARET (PEGGY) HANNUM

BY LINDA HARBRECHT

Margaret (Peggy) Haller Hannum considers herself an inveterate and uniquely experienced nest-featherer. The award-winning rug hooker has moved her family in and out of 12 homes over the course of her 52-year marriage as her husband, an United Methodist minister, earned his degrees and was reassigned to different parishes.

Each time, Peggy worked with different decorating constraints, but managed to find welcome homes for most—if not all—of the nearly 25 rugs she's hooked since she discovered the craft roughly 25 years ago.

"I planned just about each one with a particular spot in mind," said Peggy, a retired English teacher. "But no matter where I put them, they always seem to work."

When discussing her decorating technique, Peggy fails to take credit for her keen eye for combining pattern, colors, and contrasting textures within her center hall colonial-style home in Pennsylvania. Room after room offers up artful displays of treasured family antiques, and items of interest culled from a lifetime of travel.

Still, she noted, her finely honed skill was borne of necessity. "As a minister's wife, I was used to having to move from one Methodist parsonage to another," she said. "They usually weren't furnished. We were always fortunate to have some furniture we inherited, but I'd go in and make drapes, or do whatever I could to make them homey and warm."

While she and her husband, Bob, were raising their three children and Peggy was teaching school, she still managed to find a few quiet hours each evening for hooking, and found that she could complete beautiful, meaningful pieces that suited her home.

Peggy discovered rug hooking after trying her hand—and mastering—several other forms of creative expression. After completing several quilts, knitting well over a hundred sweaters, creating botanical drawings with pastels, pleating lampshades, and sewing virtually all of the window treatments, slipcovers, and bedspreads for her family's succession of homes, Peggy was encouraged to try rug hooking.

"My dear friend, Lyn Lovell, used to knit with me when we would all go on family ski vacations," she said. "One night, when we were in Killington, Vermont, she pulled out a project she was working on and said, 'I have something you're going to love.' I thought, 'I can't do one more thing,' but I tried it." She took on a small project—a hooked doorstop in a pansy pattern. "No shading, very unsophisticated—almost paint-by-number," she recalled. "But by the end of the week, I was hooked."

When she returned from vacation, Peggy ordered a catalog from the Heirloom Rug Company, and found herself captivated by it. "It was like a wish book," she said. "I couldn't wait to get started, so I called a local school, Essex Agricultural, and went to see the teacher of a class that had already started. That's how I met Meredith LeBeau, who was a wonderful, very encouraging mentor."

Meredith wanted her enthusiastic new student to start with a small project, but Peggy had already zeroed in on an iris-patterned rug that she was determined to bring to life. Soon she was well along on *Irises*, which measures 38" x 54" and currently resides in her bedroom. "I still love that rug," she says. "And I still use it. It's faded, but faded nicely."

Since that time, Peggy has perfected her skills to the point where she adapts or creates her own designs, attends regular work-

RIGHT: *The flagstone-lined foyer of Peggy's home is a gallery of her hooked rugs, cherished family photographs, and eclectic pieces of art she and her husband both inherited and collected. The central focus is* Lurcat, *a 43" x 71" Jane McGown Flynn design hooked in deep, rich tones. Hanging nearby is* Unicorn in Captivity, *a classic Pearl McGown design that she completed in 1999, and presented to her husband as a gift on their 50th anniversary. "I had done the unicorn and part of the fence, then put it away," she said. "Then I decided to finish it for my husband, and found that I actually enjoyed hooking all those picky little flowers."*

In the foreground is the Gainesborough *rug, which provides a colorful focal point in a living room awash in muted colors.*

RIGHT: *Peggy's Gainsborough rug is a 60″ round Pearl McGown design that she completed in 1983. Although it was originally designed for an earlier Federal-style home in Massachusetts, Peggy feels that its classic floral-and-scroll design adapts well to traditional furniture such as her antique corner cabinet and sidetable.*

LEFT: *Peggy's award-winning* Queen Mary, *a rug designed by Jane McGown Flynn, which measures 38″ x 72″, provides a welcome burst of color in a muted guest room. The nineteenth century walnut bed, Peggy notes, "was considered an antique when I was just a little girl." On the rocking chairs are antique dolls— one that Peggy received from her grandmother. Other accents come from a pastel created by Peggy of a lily and delphinium from her garden, and a scattering of delicately toned antique plates.*

shops on hooking and dyeing, and teaches students in the basement workshop of her home.

She's also become more prolific. When she started hooking in 1977, a rug might have taken years to complete. Now, by devoting a few hours each evening, she can complete as many as three rugs a year. Peggy primarily uses a #3-cut, which she found makes the work go much faster. "I don't have to hook as high," she said.

Her award-winning work, which has been featured several times in previous issues of *Rug Hooking* Magazine, continues to be inspired by teachers such as Nancy Blood of Oswego, N.Y., and Meredith. "I've been with Nancy in class after class for the past six years," said Peggy. "And through her unique ability, she's guided me over new horizons with color and technique. I've found that there is still so much out there to learn from other people. I've

been fortunate to have such wonderful friends and mentors."

Also evolving is her decorative style, which deftly combines old and new, traditional and obscure. Her words of advice for others hoping to do the same? "Trust your taste," she said. "Surround yourself with the things that you truly love. It will all go together."

She also offers the following:

▲ **DON'T BE OVERLY CONCERNED WITH "MATCHING" SPECIFIC RUGS TO SPECIFIC COLORS, PATTERNS OR PIECES OF FURNITURE.** Peggy pairs such seeming disparate items as Lancaster County family heirlooms, Staffordshire china, formal silver pieces, brass and copper vessels from the Mideast, Burmese tapestries, Armenian tiles, Palestinian needlework, and cherished dolls from her childhood. "Somehow," she said, "it all works."

▲ **EXPERIMENT.** "All sorts of colors and patterns work well together, even if you can't envision them," said Peggy. "Colors may complement each other in a way that you can't anticipate. The only way to find out is to move them around, and see what works with what.

"I used to make rugs for specific areas, especially when we lived in our home in Massachusetts, but I've stopped doing that. Now I want to play with the colors, not really thinking of where it has to go."

In her family room, for example, the soft, autumnal tones of her

LEFT: *Peggy's Chinese Butterflies, a Jane McGown Flynn design measuring 48" x 31", which was featured in A Celebration of Hand-Hooked Rugs XI," was selected by the 2000 National Guild of Pearl K. McGown Hookrafters to be featured on notecards. In Peggy's master bedroom, it shares space with Manchu Dragon, a 31" x 49" Jane McGown Flynn design that Peggy adapted. It was inspired, she says, by Norbert, the fierce but friendly dragon from the Harry Potter series. Nearby is a gold-washed settee, an early Pennsylvania walnut stretcher table topped with a silk runner from Burma, her mother's Lane hope chest, and a collection of antique floral plates.*

ABOVE: *Peggy's Silver Compote, which was featured in A Celebration of Hand-Hooked Rugs XII, measures 27" x 23", and was designed by Charlotte Stratton. It is given a prominent place in the Hannum dining room, where a museum-quality treatment complements the formality of antique silver tea service and cobalt-blue Staffordshire pieces atop an antique Pennsylvania blanket chest.*

RIGHT: *Peggy Hannum admits that she was probably initially attracted to this 7' x 4' rug based on its name, Salem, and originally planned to use this in an upstairs hallway in the couple's Federal-style home in Massachusetts. She began it in 1993, using all white wools that she dyed with colors supplied by her teacher, Meredith LeBeau, and finished it 11 years later.*

"One of the things Meredith taught me was to always dye enough wool for an entire project, and to keep very, very good notes," says Peggy. "I followed her advice and kept meticulous notes, so I was able to match the colors exactly when I picked the rug up again years later."

The rug takes center stage in a guest bedroom furnished with family antiques, such as a Victorian bed from her grandmother's guestroom, a marble-topped pedestal table, a Lancaster County crazy quilt her grandmother gave her when she married, and a Pennsylvania-style ladder back chair. On the bed is a quilt Peggy purchased more than 40 years ago from a Pennsylvania quilter.

ABOVE: *One of the largest rugs in the Hannum home, the 7' x 7' Wildwood design from Heirloom Rugs, echoes the warm tones of the brick hearth in the family room, and complements the copper pieces and other treasures the couple brought home from their time spent in the Middle East.*

RIGHT: *In a corner of the family room, an heirloom tavern table, antique music box, banjo and family portrait are accompanied by Peggy's Oak Scrollings rug. The 23" x 36" rug is a Jane McGown Flynn design that Peggy completed in 2002 after being inspired by tapestries she and her husband viewed in a museum in Naples.*

RIGHT: *In the living room, the Pearl McGown Ming design was hooked on a 56" by 34" rug in 2001, and sits before her father's antique Pennsylvania walnut desk in a quiet corner. Its Asian flavor provides a contrast to the traditional elegance of the formal room.*

Wildwood rug suit the warm, traditional setting. But eventually, she said, it might be replaced by *Istanbul*, which is characterized with more vivid colors and higher contrast. "I'm sure it will work fine," she said. "The beauty of hooked rugs is that they adapt so well to their surroundings."

▲ **SHOWCASE RUGS BY TONING DOWN THE BACKDROP.** Instead of layering pattern on top of pattern, Peggy likes to keep walls, floors, and window treatments fairly neutral. "That way," she said, "the rugs don't have to compete for attention."

▲ **MAKE THEM A PART OF YOUR DAILY LIFE.** With the exception of a large piece titled *Silver Compote*, which hangs in her dining room, and *Unicorn in Captivity*, which graces the foyer, most of Peggy's rugs remain underfoot.

"Rugs are rugs," she says. "You have to walk on them. I let my grandchildren play on them in the family room, and I have only one rule: Food stays in the kitchen. Other than that, the rugs are there to use and to enjoy and appreciate every day."

▲ **LOOK TO THE COLORS AND PATTERNS IN A ROOM**

FOR INSPIRATION AND A RUG TO COMPLEMENT THEM. Peggy said that when she originally began hooking rugs to fill her homes, she often looked to the distinctive shade of blue on existing wainscoting, or a prominent color in a floral pattern on the wallpaper. "Or, take your cue from one of your nicer pieces—maybe a quilt that has special significance or meaning, or a pattern on a chair you've always loved," said Peggy. "They'll point you in the right direction. Just don't be too confined by them."

▲ **EMBRACE THE UNIQUE, ALBEIT IMPERFECT, ASPECTS OF HANDMADE ITEMS.** Even an accomplished and experienced rug hooker as Peggy can see the progress in her work as she becomes more daring in color, develops a more sophisticated eye for pattern, or hones her tastes. But, as with many items in her home, each rug holds special significance and is given a worthy presentation. "Each one has its own little story to tell or has so many special memories associated with it," said Peggy. "Each one reminds me of a part of our lives, or our children's lives, or the homes we lived in. That's the joy of having them and using them." ■

Rug Hooking magazine hopes you will join us in supporting the following International Rug Hooking Guilds and Associations:

~~~~~~~~~~

Association of Traditional Hooking Artists (ATHA)

Joan Cahill, Membership Chairman
600 ¹/₂ Maple Street, Endicott, NY 13760
Phone: 607–748–7588 ✳ *E-mail: jcahill29@aol.com*

~~~~~~~~~~

The International Guild of Handhooking Rugmakers (TIGHR)

Amanda Rosser
Penbeili Mawr, Coed-y-Bryn
Llandysul, Ceredigion, SA44 5NA, Wales, UK
Phone: 44 (0) 1239 851 059 ✳ *E-mail: rospen@tiscali.co.uk*

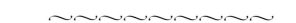

The National Guild of Pearl K. McGown Rug Hookrafters

Jenny Podlasek

25738 Polk ✳ Monee, IL 60499

Phone: 708–534-9263 ✳ *E-mail: bootscoj@famvid.com*

Check the Datebook in Rug Hooking *magazine* for a listing of Regional, State and Local Chapters and Guilds.

RUG HOOKING RESOURCES

RUG HOOKING RESOURCES

RUG HOOKING RESOURCES

About The Sponsors

OUR BEGINNINGS

In the 150 years since rug hooking made its way to North America, no periodicals covered the subject until professional rug designer Joan Moshimer began publishing *Rug Hooker News & Views* in 1972, a newsletter "by and for rug hookers." But as more people took up the craft and the rug hooking industry flourished, it became apparent that only a full-fledged magazine could best serve the growing audience.

In 1989, Stackpole Inc., a Pennsylvania-based book and magazine publisher, transformed Joan's newsletter into *Rug Hooking,* the only full-color, internationally read magazine devoted exclusively to the subject of hand-hooked rugs.

AN INSIDE LOOK AT RUG HOOKING MAGAZINE

Rug Hooking brings its readers striking color photographs of gorgeous rugs and stories that both inspire and instruct. Each issue of *Rug Hooking* contains articles on dyeing, color planning, designing, hooking techniques, rug hooking history, and more. Feature articles cover topics ranging from elaborate Orientals to country-style primitives.

The magazine's departments include *Dear Beginning Rug Hooker,* which presents a step-by-step project from a leading designer. Readers can follow the lesson plan, then hook their own rug using the *free pattern* included in the issue. *Recipes from the Dye Kitchen,* contains dyeing tips and formulas. *Reader's Gallery* exhibits one accomplished rug hooker's body of work. *Teacher Feature* lets readers in on a noted teacher's classroom lessons. *Elements* focuses on a specific design element or technique. *Beyond Our Borders* introduces rug hookers to other fiber arts, such as braiding and appliqué, which can be used to enhance hooked pieces.

In addition to instructional columns, issues of *Rug Hooking* contain *Date Book,* an engagement calendar listing events, classes, and gatherings; *Camps & Workshops,* profiling a rug school; and *The Loop,* linking rug hookers with each other.

BOOKS FROM RUG HOOKING

In addition to publishing five issues of the magazine each year, *Rug Hooking* also publishes books, of which *A Celebration of Hand-Hooked Rugs* is one. Through the years *Celebration* has brought hundreds of beautiful rugs to the attention of rug hookers worldwide. *Rug Hooking's pattern books* give new and advanced rug hookers patterns and detailed instructions from talented designers. Our *Sourcebook* is a reference guide for those looking for suppliers, teachers, workshops, and guilds.

The Framework Series was introduced in 1998 with the publication of *People and Places: Roslyn Logsdon's Imagery in Fiber,* written by one of the most influential teachers in the rug hooking world. *Recipes From the Dye Kitchen,* the second book in the series, was based on Maryanne Lincoln's magazine column. Other books include *Preserving the Past in Primitive Rugs* by designer Barbara Brown; *A Rug Hooker's Garden,* in which ten experts teach how to hook a bouquet of blossoms; *The Pictorial Rug* by Jane Halliwell, an introduction to hooking a picture with wool; *The Complete Natural Dyeing Guide* by Marie Sugar, offers 89 natural dye recipes with natural ingredients; *Hooking with Yarn* by Judy Taylor; and our latest book *Hooked on the Wild Side* by Elizabeth Black, a recognized expert on hooking animals, both domestic and wild.

Our most recent books include *Basic Rug Hooking,* a compilation of 12 beginners projects and directions on design, color planning, wool selection, and hooking techniques, plus exclusive pull-out patterns; *The Secrets of Finishing Hooked Rugs* by Margaret Siano, which offers complete directions for each finishing technique; and *The Secrets of Primitive Hooked Rugs* by Barbara Carroll, who takes you step-by-step through the process of creating a full-size Wooly Horse pattern.

Books and magazines aren't the only way we communicate with the rug hooking community. Our *web site* (www.rughook ingonline.com) is packed with vivid photos, informative text, and links to other helpful sites.

Rug Hooking's objective is to be the primary source of information and inspiration for rug hookers of all levels of experience. Since 1989 we have met that objective, and we intend to continue to do that for all the diverse and talented rug hookers found throughout the world. ∎